How to get over a boy in 6 weeks

8 stages to forget a Jerk or cheating ex who hurts you.

How to deal with a crush's rejection or ghosting from a lover.

Healing toxic thoughts from different break-ups.

Eliza Bayles

Table Of Content

STAGE 4

STAGE 5

STAGE 6

STAGE 7

STAGE 8

STAGE 1

Know when it's not working out: Try, but never too hard

"

It is very normal to love, and it's not a crime to fall in love; the problem is when you fall in love with someone who treats you as an option. Everyone deserves to be treated as a priority by the person we love; when this treatment is mutual and reciprocal, we call it true love. But when we find ourselves in a situation where we treat someone as the top priority but get treated with less value in return, our natural response may be to find out why we're not being loved as much as we love the other person and make adjustments where necessary.

However, in certain situations, even though our feeling says otherwise, it is the best decision to let go of our emotions for the other person and let them be.This could be very difficult as it brings emotional and psychological strain on us which raises the question of how far we should go for unrequited love. How do we determine whether to push a little harder to get the mutual love of the other person or to disregard our feelings and consider it a lost battle not worth fighting?

Relationship or liking someone deserves little effort on your part. In essence, nothing is worth the effort more than your love. So work for it. Even when a relationship may not work out, trying for it is the first step you need to take. Make an effort to deserve the love you are after; let your partner see reason with. Remember you like him first, and sometimes it is your duty to get him to where you are emotionally before judging that they aren't reciprocating.

"Love may take its tools on your partner. Sometimes, the person you like didn't hate you; he is just not in the right state of mind to love you back at the moment. The key to trying for your love is that you get a chance to make it work. Every little effort matters."

Note that you need to be wary of trying too hard. Trying too hard tends to push you too hard; hence, you may end up breaking yourself. Take time to fathom what to do and what not to do. For example, when it is not working out, most of us find it hard to reconcile with that fact and stop taking extreme measures to prove our self-worth. But the truth is, he may be in love with a lady not as beautiful as you are, or probably not as curvy, sexy, intelligent, or fun to be with, so while trying to improve on your beauty just to catch his attention, or your posture or disposition, choose your ways carefully. Where you are not too sure what to do, the guide below should help put your thoughts together.

Be aware of the signs of a one-sided attraction

The attraction may start as a one-sided feeling, and absolutely nothing is bad about this. It only goes wrong when the attraction is not reciprocated for a long time. This is why you need to understand your stand in a relationship. Perhaps you are in a one-sided relationship or love affairs unconsciously. People are different, and it indeed takes some time for some guys to truly catch feelings. Especially when this guy is most of a playboy and feels less concerned about commitment or responsibilities, he will enjoy the moment with you, but he might not be a "dating" type of guy. Though you might think that this is not an excuse for someone you love to treat you as badly, the truth is sometimes we love the wrong guys.

Trying for your love starts from identifying that it is one-sided. You have no one to blame for falling in love with them. No one has the right to blame you for falling in love; not even you have the right to condemn your emotion. You have no control over how you feel and how you will feel in a few months or years to come. So, accept your feelings for what they are; if the other party isn't reciprocating, it is safe and smart to believe they are not there yet. Do not rush it; just accept the fact that it is one-sided at the moment.

What are the signs of a one-sided attraction?

• *It is one-sided if you are the only one with positive energy*

- *If you are often left alone in your relationship*

- *If the other person does not show affection to you*

- *When your crush finds you as a mere classmate or a colleague*

- *When it is obvious you are giving but not getting anything back.*

Knowing that your relationship is one-sided is the first step to take when a relationship is not working out or when your crush is not reciprocating. This will help put things in better perspective; you will know what to do and where your partner is. While this is your first step for trying for your love, it is also a step for moving on. Knowing that it is one-sided does not only make you try more; it also makes you understand that you may expect nothing in return. Trying and giving doesn't necessarily mean that you get back. However, knowing that you try for your love will put your mind at ease and clearly define that what is not working is just not working and not because you did not deserve it.

Know that you can't force mutual feeling

"It takes two to tangle" After you determine that your relationship is one-sided, it is essential to know that you cannot force mutual feeling. It is understandable that for a working relationship, both parties must be involved; it is one thing that your partner doesn't love you enough; it is another that your partner does not love you at all. In the process of working for your love, always remember that you cannot force the other person to love. Know that no one has control over how they feel. So, trying to get them into a stable emotional place where they can see how much you care and reciprocate does not mean you should force them to love you.

"Appreciate it when someone naturally falls in love with you; it doesn't matter who likes who first; all that matters is the fact you love someone who sees reasons to also love you back. That is enough."

Furthermore, forcing someone to like you is like admitting that they do not love you. In my experience, nobody forcefully stays in a relationship. Understanding that he doesn't reciprocate your love can help you make better decisions. Knowing that it is impossible to make someone feel what he does not feel for you will make you select your choices wisely. It is possible that you are already close to him; you may even be best friends or talk mates. Whatever choices you make, be smart enough to understand that it may not necessarily arouse the emotion you want.

• Dress well/ try looking more attractive

Good and nice clothes portray a better message of your personality, they can even win some affections. The best way to get someone to love you is to look super attractive and comfortable. Remember, no one will appreciate you for looking shabby. However, you need to put it at the back of your mind that no one can choose how you dress. Define your fashion sense; wear something you admire on yourself and feel comfortable in. Know that if the relationship does work out, you do not want to stay uncomfortable to stay in love.

"Looking good is not just for the other person. It is for you. Look more attractive but never sacrifice your comfort for attractiveness. The truth lies in how genuine you appear to yourself. How comfortable you can carry those sexy dresses. Remember, your clothing is part of who you so thread carefully. Never throw caution into the air. This is a relationship where we do not guarantee a positive outcome; you do not want to lose who you really are in the process of looking good. Wear makeup if you love it, do everything that makes you more attractive, but let them be things that sit well with your personality and not something that put you all out unnecessarily."

Consider some skin work. You do not want to look all dry and rough beside your partner. The first thing to know why how you look matters is by reflecting on the appearance of your crush. Loving someone, at first sight, takes more than words; they need to look cute for you to be drawn uncontrollably to them. It is by nurturing this feeling that you get to know them better. You start to learn about them, and then you find them even more interesting to stay with. So, work on your skin as well; you do not need to remove all imperfections or flaws. Get yourself a well-moisturized skin. Good and healthy skin is for you because you will love yourself even more.

The way we dress tells so much generally about us and has an effect on how people feel about us. According to psychologists, the way we dress determines how attractive people find us. The person you love must find you attractive, this triggers the hormones of affection in them, and if they really love you too, they will reciprocate and love to look their best when you are together or likely to meet. In fact, a person may have feelings for you and eventually start ignoring you if you dress shabbily. Your dress also impacts your perception and acceptance in social circles, are you smartly dressed enough to be presented before your friends? You need to pay some attention to his social circle and make sure you're well-dressed enough to fit in his circle, and a man may decide not to openly complain about your dress so as not to hurt your feelings. He may, however, try to avoid you or avoid meeting with you so as not to cause him embarrassment among his friends and colleagues. It is up to you to realize and work on this fact.

Having said the above, exercise absolute control over how you look, what you wear, and what you do. I am a comfy dresser; if the cloth is not comfortable, I'm not wearing it. But I've learned to look super cute for myself, and maybe when next I find myself a little crush, he will love that too. Self-love is an integral part of getting people to love you; they've got to know that you love yourself even more. And your value lies in your ability to love yourself, understand what fashion looks to you and what attractiveness means to you.

• Don't try to be someone you're not

Here is a simple and subtle reminder that you must not lose yourself in the process of getting someone to love you. Before anyone, you know yourself the most; you understand things that make you who you are. You know what feels comfortable. You do not need to start clubbing hard just because your crush will turn up at every party. Do things gradually, learn to go at your own pace, do not rush things, and do not let anyone rush you.

"The good thing about never losing who you are is that just in case your crush reciprocates, you can be rest assured that he falls in love with you and not some unknown personality. So do not change you."

However, it is vital to learn to separate what makes you who you are from things that are merely flaws. No one is born with a rude personality, and you chose those. So, you must do away with things that make you appear rude, careless, and inconsiderate. For example, suppose you work in the same office or go to the same school, you do not want to be tagged "RUDE BITCH" by other people around you and expect someone to fall in love with you. Try being a positive and warm person. Captivate the one you love from natural acts of love and kindness.

Before you seek love, spread it. No one needs you to render help to everyone around you, but being a bad person isn't a flaw people have to deal with for you. Check yourself to learn about things you do that are just toxic to people around you.

Understand that people have feelings too, and you have no right to treat anyone with disdain. Let your heart learn to appreciate people for a lot of other reasons. See humanity in everyone and do good things to people. This has nothing to do with who you love; carrying bad energy or intentionally hurting people occasions a lot of harm to who you are. Change your ways if you find out you are in this situation. It is never too late to be good and reciprocate kindness. Pay attention to the little things that make the world a beautiful place. Even if your love didn't work out, you might realize you have already found ways to heal naturally.

You can do anything to get the attention of a partner you love but never try so hard as to pretend to be a person you're not. Remain confident in the person you are; remain yourself. Never allow your affection to make you behave in ways that are contrary to your values, don't go the extra length to sound more fun, you don't need to take a loan to buy a beautiful dress; in fact, never go to the extent of borrowing dresses and shoes from friends just to satisfy a guy, you need to be your natural self, he needs to love the person you are, it's not your business to create the person he'll love in yourself.

• Take notice of the red flags you've been ignoring

Do not make the mistake of thinking your partner is perfect. In reality, no one is perfect, not even you. Hence, look out for the red flags. Know things you cannot tolerate. Check out for the flaws you cannot handle and the ways of life that didn't sit well with you. However, do not give up on someone for their flaws; if you love them enough, then you have to believe that your love has the power to change and heal them too.

So, if your partner has bad habits, you should not let go quickly. If your crush has flaws, you do not need to give up on them for that, but never forget to take cognizance of those flaws. Red flags are indeed helpful during the relationship and even if the love didn't work out. When you love someone whose flaws are known to you, if he doesn't reciprocate, you can set your mind at ease for not having to deal with all of those bad behaviors. However, if your relationship does work out, you know where to start making him a better person.

Now is the right time to take notice of specific things you may have been ignoring. Emotion seems to make us blind to certain realities; this is why people say love is blind. Have you been giving too much, just to get the attention of this person that you hardly see anything bad in him? It could be anything but do not be unreasonable. No one wants a nagging girlfriend. Understand that your role in his life is not to be his mom. However, if he truly needs help, you will find a place to get him there.

- ## Check your character

Are you in love with the person you are not showing love to? No one can read down in your heart to know what you truly feel. However, we show people that we care a lot about them by treating them well. Showing them a better us. Check how you relate to your crush; can he even guess that you love him at all. Have you tried being friends with him? If you are his friend already, are you staying in that zone carelessly? Love needs courage. It is courage that will make your love work. You have to show the other person that you love him.

Without doing anything that makes you uncomfortable, how about building your character a little bit this time. Good character is worth more than money. How warm are you naturally to people? Ask yourself, what kind of person are you?

"Find answers from things around you, what your loved ones think about you. You do not need to pay attention to what everyone thinks about you, but your friends' opinion matters a lot. Do not change who you are carelessly. I know it can be hard picking attributes that make you who you are from those that are just flawed. However, by determining the kind of person you want to be, the kind of person you are comfortable with, you can find the answers to eliminate your flaws and admire imperfections."

Remember that you are a unique person, not made to be perfect for anyone. Moreover, your lovers have to see your imperfection and love you with it. Do not be perfect for anyone, for love lies in the ability of your boyfriend or crush to accept you for who you are and not who you are trying to be.

STAGE 2

Have a frank physical discussion

"

Whether you need to express your feelings for a guy or are already in a relationship where the guy has failed to express love and show you that he cares about you just like you care about him, or you are contemplating breaking up with a partner who persistently cheats. It all starts from the communication.

As a woman, you need to know that communicating how you feel in every situation is not bad, and you do not need to feel inferior. So, if you sometimes feel like only the guy should express himself, or only the guy should demand fair treatment in a relationship, you are setting yourself up for heartbreaks, unequal treatment, and bottled emotions.

I really advise that you speak up instead of bottling up your feelings. Not knowing where you truly belong will negatively impact your mental health and keep brewing false hopes in you. It is very easy to want to love someone till they naturally realize how much you love them. However, not talking may also mean watching the guy you love go into a relationship with another girl.

- Don't be scared to express how you feel

The reason why your love is not working out may be because you've failed to express yourself. Loving someone takes a lot of energy; however, having the courage to express yourself requires more energy. Taking the step of starting a frank discussion may be the salvation your love needs.

Sometimes, we think we are expressing love, but we may not be doing it enough. The other person may be getting the wrong impression. Sometimes, it is even possible that they know nothing about that precious feeling you treasure so much for them. The good thing about speaking up and telling someone how you feel about them is that you may end up finding out that they feel the same way about you. However, you two are delaying the progress by keeping the feelings to yourself.

"Aside from the fact that the ability to speak up may improve your relationship, one of the beauties of a woman is taking control of how she feels and assuming the courage to speak up and express herself. Loving someone takes some gut, and you have no reason to feel shy about how you feel."

The best way to deal with your emotion is to own it. Own every part of it, and don't let it take full control. Express your feeling boldly and confidently, knowing that rejection is not the end of your journey. Expect rejection but keep positivity alive because it will make you express yourself better.

Sometimes, you've got to prove to the person you love that you deserve to be with them.

If you are already in a relationship, speaking up and expressing how you truly feel, will make you have a reasonable level of control. Understand that you do want to keep your feelings all to yourself. If your partner is not reciprocating with the same energy, speaking about it may help clear any misconception and tells you where you are actually standing.

"It is important to know that just because the energy isn't equal yet does not mean that your boyfriend isn't in love with you as much as you are in love with him. However, people progress in the relationship at different paces. So do not sum up the lack of full emotion, and do not interpret his lack of words for hatred; speak about it. Learn about how your partner feels in words and not in your judgment."

Often, the relationship is not working the way we want it because we fail to speak about how badly it hurts when the other person does not reciprocate with equal energy. Sometimes, you've got to demand the love you are giving, and by talking it out, you may realize the reason why your crush or boyfriend is not where you are emotionally.

"Physical communication, not online chat, and text messages are the basis of a good relationship. So, whether your relationship works, or you have your crush

loving you back, or you just get to be done with the feeling and work on moving on, it all depends on how fast you are able to make peace with the fact that communication is indispensable for your feeling."

Whether you are in a relationship or you have a crush on someone, failure to communicate how you actually feel will make it impossible to know what the other person feels unless he decides to talk about it. In a relationship, a lot of disagreement is occasioned by what is not said or what is not properly said. Hence, it is impossible to have a workable relationship without mastering the art of talking about your affection.

• Speak as clearly as you can

When expressing yourself, there is an ultimate need that you state your feeling as clear as possible. If you have a request, demand an answer clearly to know where the relationship is going and what the other person feels about you.

If you are set to talk to your crush, you may express yourself in ways that did not put your all out and still confirm how they feel about you. However, this may not be perfect in all ramifications. For example, asking your crush to be your friend may be quicker than asking him on a date. On some occasions, he is possibly interested in being a friend with you and not interested in being your boyfriend. Hence, clarity is the key.

If you are already in a relationship, express how you feel about him and let him know how much you miss the affection he is not giving. Make him understand that you are ready to hear his side of the story. This is because some people just lack the way to express emotions.

Speaking may also allow you to know more about what your boyfriend or crush is going through. Do not stop loving before you are certain of what the other person feels. You do not want to hear about how much they love you just when you start moving on.

I learned that not talking will not do you any good. I recall how a friend, Lisa found herself in a toxic relationship. She gave all she could to this handsome boyfriend; however, he wasn't reciprocating the feelings. She really did sacrifice a lot for the relationship to work. Unfortunately, she was missing out on expressing herself. Because of the lack the courage to hear that her boyfriend didn't care much about her, she couldn't really talk about how much it hurt to be in unrequited love. Spending countless nights weeping, expecting a call that won't come, and waiting for replies to her message till she slept off every night. This happens almost every day just after four months of starting the relationship.

Ironically, the relationship started all lovey-dovey, so it was hard to tell what was going on in her boyfriend's mind. She was losing so much than she could bear, and slowly she was getting drowned in that toxic relationship. Each day, she had to give up things like her principles, integrity, and personal standards, and slowly she lost herself. Eventually, the discussion she was avoiding became the only necessary thing that remained to keep the goal of the relationship clear. The frank conversation revealed the fact that her boyfriend stopped loving her six months ago. However, he was not able to tell her this. She was confronted with the bitter truth she had been avoiding long after she had given up on several things.

This shows that not talking will notsave your relationship from crumbling, but perhaps you are trying too hard to keep a broken relationship together.

The situation is similar even if you have a crush on a boy and you are not sure what he feels about you. Expressing yourself is the only way to stop falling too hard and expecting him to reciprocate. It is also the key to knowing that he feels the same way. Your situation becomes clearly defined, and know that this will do more good than harm even when the boy does not feel the same way.

Try to find out from the other person's perspective. Understand that not everyone will love you back. This will create a setting ground where you learn to appreciate how someone honestly feels about you. We've all got to deal with the fact that sometimes, we would love someone who, for some reason, just doesn't feel the same as we do. It may be because of their current situation, and sometimes, he may think you are too much for him. When you are talking with your crush or partner, understand that they have the right to have different views and to feel differently about you.

Communication can be imperfect depending on how you are able to convey your feelings accurately. However, not talking at all is terrible. One can easily understand what Jean-Paul Sartre meant when she stated that lack of communication is the source of all violence. You can avoid anger, and you can avoid hating someone if you start the conversation. This is because talking about it will reveal the facts you know nothing about. You have to master the act of communicating accurately and get accustomed to talking about your feelings. If you are not getting right at expressing yourself, then learn to improve your communication skills. Believe me, and this is going to have a lot of impact on your other relationships.

Sometimes we are not communicating because we do not dare to talk, but we are not sure what to talk about. Identifying your feeling is just as important as the feeling itself. Hence, it is essential not to make a hasty generalization about what you feel. Take time to understand the emotion and distill it to know if this is true love or mere likeness. Sometimes, you may just like the person you think you love. This is why in some relationships, the first person to call it off is the same person who initiated the relationship in the beginning. After distilling your feeling, it becomes easier to talk about them.

"Not expressing myself clearly in a relationship made me realize that I wasn't standing up for myself. I wasn't

demanding how to be fairly treated. It made me realize how much I work for a relationship that does not have my interest in it. It was all about what the other person feels or thinks. This is taking me nowhere, but I never knew. Not so long enough, it became clear that if a relationship fails because of honest communication, it is because it never truly exists to begin with."

- ## Learn to see things from his perspective

Do not sum up the lack of feeling of hatred. He may not love you right now, but that doesn't naturally mean that he hates you. The truth is people have different reasons for not falling in love. For some, it is a bad experience from an EX. Sometimes it is merely because you really do not fit the picture they want, and sometimes it is because you are just too awesome for some of them to deal with. You have to tell yourself that whatever anyone feels about you is not your fault. However, it is also essential to know that you can see things from their point of view. Even if this does not give you the relationship you wanted, you may understand why it is not working and move on quickly.

Loving someone can be a little tricky; you run the risk of them not loving you back. However, since we cannot control our hearts, it becomes essential to let the feelings flow and accept what will be and what will not.

Seeing things from others perspective also allows you to view things differently. What is not a big deal to you may mean a lot to another. You may quickly realize why you should not be with this person and find easy peace in your heart. But all of these will remain impossible till you decide to listen to their side of the story.

Loving is listening, and you want to hear them out; you want to understand your partner even more. This is what talking will get you only if you understand that this is not about you alone. It is about two persons. So, if your boyfriend isn't reciprocating, you should hear him too.

- ## Stop making excuses for his behavior

Making excuses for him will only hurt you more. The more excuses you make, the more you will live and believe a lie, a state of mind that does not exist. The first state in moving on is understanding that not everyone knows the worth of a rare Gem, which you're. Not everyone will feel exactly the way you feel, and not everyone deserves to be with you. You deserve so much more than someone who is not ready to love you back.

Therefore, understanding someone before they express themselves is wrong. Never make excuses for why someone may not be loving you. One bad thing about making excuses is that it keeps you expecting more. Also, it will be stopping you from expressing yourself and know where he really is. You keep thinking you understand him, whereas you do not.

The reason why you are making so many excuses is that you are running away from hearing the truth. It is because you are afraid of hearing that he does not feel the same way. It is because you are not happy to watch your relationship break apart after so much energy and commitment. And if you are afraid right here, it is understandable. You have every right to be scared, and you have every right to want your relationship to work. However, more than wanting your relationship to work and expecting that someone loves you back, you have the right to remain whole again; you have the right to stand firm and true to your feelings, and you have the right to move from a bad relationship to a healthy one. So do not make an excuse.

In the long run, you will realize that you understand him and make excuses for him because you want to build a relationship that is not meant to work. If your partner is inconsistent or not reciprocating, you will realize that it is not generally because of work or exhaustion. If he has a change of mind about the relationship, you will find out that it has nothing to do with you. No one wants to face the hurt that comes from a broken relationship. But sometimes, it is what we all need to experience to know what true love looks like and feels like.

Second Week (How moving on starts)

STAGE 3

If communication fails

Case I: Dealing with rejection or heartbreak

It was pleasing when I heard a breakup coach and dating expert, Natalia Juarez, saying that "We've all been on both sides of this equation in our lives. There's no shame in it," She further noted that though things may have never materialized into a formal relationship, learning that someone doesn't share the same feelings you have for them can make you feel the same sting associated with heartbreak. "It's still a disappointment in love. It's still heartbreak. And it's all part of the process of finding your right person or people."

"I'm a huge fan of expressing my emotion, so I do not know how to hold back when I love someone; I just find the time and say it. Sharing your heart with the guy you're crushing on is worth it; you do not want to regret

*not saying when you see him with another girl forever.
You probably even think she is not that cute. However, if
such communication fails, understand that it is not your
fault. Natalia has something to say on this. In her words,
"If you're disappointed, just let the person know. You can
say, 'I'm really disappointed to hear that; I might need a
few weeks to recover, but I know I'll be fine again soon."*

Another thing to know is that you are not alone; people have
gone through and successfully emerged from this exact
situation stronger. A fellow shared an experience, and she
said it's the most shocking of her several experiences of
rejection. She met a guy called Jack through an online dating
site, and both kept constant communication for about a
month. Jack lived in LA, but he liked her; he was self-
employed and had a flexible schedule, so the distance wasn't
a problem. They both finally took it to the next level and
spoke on the phone. Their first phone call was six hours! She
is someone who really doesn't enjoy talking on the phone,
except people calling for an emergency, she rarely uses her
phone. If she gets a call, she looks for ways to end the
conversation as quickly as possible. But the case of Jack was
different; they both enjoyed talking to each other and finding
out all about themselves. My friend said Jack was cool and
exciting, and he always sounded awesome over the phone.
They finally set a date, and she was very optimistic about it;
she was already fantasizing about a bi-coastal cruise,
spending time in LA with her newfound love, and then back
to NYC. She was pleased about the possibilities. In her own

words, "I felt like something really special was brewing…" and she became eager to see how it would all unfold. They had another phone conversation that went well but probably wasn't as cool as the previous ones. It only lasted an hour and a half because his friends unexpectedly showed up, and he had to cut the conversation short. She had a feeling something was a little off, but she ignored those feelings.

A few days later, she was on the phone with a Time warner guy over some cable issues when she got an email from Jack. She was excited to open it, and this was the content:

Hey Sabrina,
"It's been great getting to know you and Talking the past few days, but unfortunately, I don't think I'm the best match for you, and I think you deserve to have the person who is best for you. You're an awesome person who I definitely connect but it's more on a friendship level."
All the best and enjoy Italy.

She said she lost the ability to speak, the Time Warner man asked her if the connection finished loading, and she couldn't answer. It was like she was in a fog; she was shocked and couldn't believe Jack could ditch her that way. She felt terrible, especially the thought that they never really met, and he concluded he's not a match; at least he could have met her before dumping her. She became upset and felt like an idiot; how could she be so crazy about a guy she never met. This is just a glimpse of feelings you need to face when a guy you love isn't into you; in this instance, he didn't even give a chance for better communication before concluding that he's not a match; this isn't just a case of failed communication but collapsed communication, he had nursed prejudiced and hastily acted on it, but she had to move on with life if she didn't move on, she wouldn't be telling us this story.

The first stage in getting ready for a relationship is knowing you are not into a game, so you can't always have a win-win situation in it. While it is good not to give up merely because things are not working out, it is equally important to know when to quit and move on. Hope is not always beautiful; there is false hope and you must never be afraid of giving up on false hope. Lay down your hope for him by making an intentional decision never to seek out for him again. One of such situations where you must quit and move on is after communication bears no fruit. You don't need to subject yourself to pain in the hope that things will be better in the future you have no control over. You need to ask yourself, 'What if it never does?' The best you can do is reconcile with the bitter truth, no matter how painful it might be. After having an open conversation with someone you love but who doesn't seem to share the same feelings with you, you may feel that something is wrong with you because of this rejection, but the fact is that the reason your crush turned you down may not have anything to do with you. Remember that unreciprocated love may be hurting the other person as well. You may believe that your pain is the only thing in the universe if you are rejected at first. Research shows, however, that the guy who does not return your love is most likely hurt too. Real men don't like inflicting pain on women.

You should know that you develop emotional strength and self-confidence through this experience. A rejection is not the friendliest approach to improve these abilities, but you're going to become stronger if you focus on learning rather than wailing. You can even comprehend your emotional wants and needs better. There are countless reasons why they chose to act like this. It is not your duty to speculate on these reasons. They may not be ready to enter into a relationship, or some personal things are happening in their life that requires special attention, or they might think they feel optimistic about you, but the moment is not right. Never engage in the desperate task of finding out why you're not good enough for him.

A friend shared an experience sometimes back; there was a girl he met in school, and he truly loved her cheerful and free nature. He said her charisma was what got him attracted to her more, and good enough, she approached him, introduced herself, and politely requested his contact. He was filled with ecstasy because he said he'd never seen a more cheerful and bold lady in his life. She started calling to check on him regularly and started messaging him online, he knew she was in love, and he was attracted to her too, but this was a period he was struggling with a lot of problems in his life. His dad was dying of cancer, his mom left home and never returned, and he was struggling to meet up with both his school fee and his father's medical bills; in his own words, he said his life was "enveloped in sadness" and because of this, he couldn't reciprocate the vibes he was getting from the girl. In her usual charismatic manner, the girl walked up to him and told him her true feelings in a frank discussion; he told her he had feelings too but would love to be left alone for the time being. Still, she wouldn't agree, she promised to stick by him all through his travails on the condition that he loves her back immediately, she immediately became a burden in his eye, and he blocked all communications with her.

This settles my first rejection. Seeing from the guys' perspective made me realize it is not always because you are not enough. Sometimes, it is because the situation isn't right. This made me realize that rejection after an honest discussion is ok. If your crush needs that space, he is entitled to it. It will pain you and be hard for a while, but not for life.

I commend your bravery to speak to him and taking control of your emotion. Believe me, and it is not a simple thing to do for the weak-minded. It is sad to hear that things did not work out with both of you, but I'm pleased to tell you it's never the end of life for you. What you need to do to continue your happy life:

o   Stay positive to yourself

It all starts with your mindset; staying positive is a daily effort that takes focus and attention. You must be purposeful about being optimistic if you're going to overcome the brain's inclination to focus on rejection. You need to admit that the problem is not you but him. To learn to focus on the positive, you need to know how to eliminate negative self-talk. The more negative thinking you ruminate, the more power you give your negative emotions. Once you get rid of self-defeating and negative thoughts, it's time to help your brain learn what you want it to focus on - the positive things. You are good, and you are beautiful, you are perfectly made, you're not inferior, neither is he superior to you, you are just okay enough for whoever is ready to appreciate your worth truly; you are priceless and invaluable.

You don't have to nurse grudges and pain, neither should you plan to treat him rudely; this makes your heart free from unnecessary thoughts and helps you keep an open-minded and positive mindset. Determine to be polite and don't hold any malice against him; all these aides your positivity and helps you evade negative emotions. The act of positive thinking will come naturally after some time, but first, you have to give yourself a little help by consciously selecting something positive to think about.

Getting rejected is almost like getting broken up with – except instead of mourning something you lost, you mourn something you never got to have. You need to realize you've not lost anything, you never had him, and life doesn't end there. Another thing that affects positivity is hoping he'll change his mind, the reason is that each time you think about him and refuse to embrace the realities, and you daydream about being together and wonder whether he would suddenly understand that you are a good choice for him. Each time you think this way and he doesn't come forth, you sink deeper in negativity; as long as you're hoping this way, you're never going to get over him, and you'll never do your heart the needed help in getting healed on time.

o   Respect his decision and speak positively about him

Embrace the refusal as early as possible. Studies have revealed that the quicker you accept the refusal and try to go on, the simpler this difficult period will be for you. It also means that you develop emotional strength against possible future reoccurrence. In case it happens with another guy, you will never be left devastated. You need to respect his sincerity towards you, he could have decided to play you or deceive you probably to keep you as a sex object, but rather he came out plain, you need to appreciate this fact. Once your crush has honestly revealed his true feelings for you, and it was not what you hoped for, you need to be strong enough to accept the reality. You would only be fooling yourself if you keep thinking that it could not be true, and one day you would hear that it was a lie or prank. You must avoid forcing yourself on the guy, and you must not stalk or bug him because it could turn out creepy and annoying. Give him space and respect his privacy decision. As you can't force yourself to love someone, you need to understand that he also has no control over how he truly feels. Even if this feels like a stupid decision for him, you've got to let it go.

"Do not consider yourself insufficient or not deserving of love. The more you press on your feelings, the more likely

he would dislike you as it is a big turn-off for guys. Know that one of the best ways to heal fast is accepting that rejection is part of life. Persistently blaming yourself will breed a lack of confidence, which in turn will make moving on with your life very difficult. Your greatest way out is to build your confidence by not taking your failed love adventure too personally; the bottom line is never to blame yourself."

Lack of confidence makes you unable to move on with your life, ask another boy out, or build a better relationship with some other guy. Your biggest option is to boost your confidence in this sense. And the best way to do that is to quit taking your failed relationship too personally or blaming yourself. Every person has surely experienced getting rejected in one way or another during their lifetime; your case is not an exception. Accepting this will help you heal faster and make you more emotionally mature since you can let go easier. If possible, you may continue to be friends with your crush. If he hasn't told you to stay away from him, and you still have to meet with him regularly, then continue to be mere friends. Treat him with respect just like how you would treat every other ordinary people around you. However, you need to be careful and not let emotion override your logic; that is; you need to know your limits and control your passion. Just be as friendly and courteous as you would be to others.

Learn not to harbor any hatred or bitterness towards him. In the real sense, he has no duty or responsibility to love you back. The fact that you love someone doesn't mean they will love you too. We all can't control this emotion. So do away with the entitlement feeling and understand that he has the right to say 'no' to you just like everyone else.

Never allow yourself to fall into the trap of saying mean things about the guy to make yourself feel better. This type of thinking can ultimately make you feel even more bitter and angry rather than helping you heal. Feeling angry towards him may occur, but anger is usually obsessive. Try to wish them all the best. If you genuinely love him you want to see him happy always, even if it's not with you. Resist the urge to become angry. If you slander the guy in front of others, it means you still have him deep in your thoughts; therefore, anger will trap you in your anguish instead of letting you free.

You need to cut unessential calls, emails, and unnecessary bumping into them. In the healing process, you need to give reasonable communication distance, which may be more difficult if you are workmates and classmates or you need to be together someplace every day. In that case, you must cut your interactions with those essential to achieving your common interest. Do your best to keep the conversation light. A lengthy conversation runs the risk of building up new, emotional connections between you, which may eventually lead to rejection a second time. If you attend the same class, plan to be elsewhere straight after class or work so you won't have to worry about having an uncomfortable little conversation with him.

You don't need to discomfort yourself to avoid the guy, but make sure you don't intentionally look for them; in other words, you don't need to make elaborate plans to avoid him, and it should rather be strictly, discreet and natural. You must also do away with gossiping about him, and people will voice their opinion about what has transpired, don't let them drag you into that. If you allow gossipers to drag you back into his matter, your mind would not be focused on positivity, and you might unintentionally nurse secret pains that will keep you heartbroken. You don't need to add fuel to the burning furnace of rumors, be firmly dismissive or defensive when confronted by nosy friends, draw a red line by making them understand it is your personal life, and you won't tolerate intrusions. When you're amidst friends who offer you emotional support by abusing the guy, make sure you change the subject. Whatever you say won't change their minds, so always be the bigger person, smile and be polite.

o   Never lose your self-esteem

Ending your relationship or one that never actually started can be damaging to your self-esteem. Therefore, you must strive to do things that make you feel good about yourself. You must seek out self-improvement strategies to help uphold your confidence. One of the hardest parts about getting rejected or heartbroken is that it's entirely out of your control. Complicated circumstances have a bright side as well, and they may set us on the correct road if we make the most effective use of bad situations in life. But that can only happen if we are heading that way. You must stop embracing your bad emotions, and lamenting will not help. Never permit pessimist sentiments like, "All guys stink, my life sucks, I'm not that lucky." It just adds to your unhappiness and denies your life joy. Do not blame yourself for the decision of anyone else. You have no control over how he feels, or what he wants to do, or whether he'll change his mind. And that kind of lack of control can leave you feeling depressed and not in control of your own life. So, the best thing to do right now is to get over a guy who doesn't like you back or is not treating you right. This begins with yourself, your sense of esteem, the same way you feel about yourself.

Understanding that a guy turning you down is never a reflection of your worth. Don't mistake such lack of love for personal failure. You must ensure nothing breaks your inherent self-worth. Remember that before this guy's opinion ever meant much to you, you were your own distinct and intriguing person. The more you remember and act on this, the stronger and more beautiful you will feel. A guy's feeling about you is not a verdict on your character. Just because a guy isn't interested in a relationship with you or does not want to keep what you had does not mean your status as a unique, fantastic individual has diminished! It's very typical to feel sad that your crush or boyfriend probably doesn't appreciate how great you are, but this should never make you see yourself as worthless.

When a guy rejects your love, you must realize that he rejected the request and not you. Nobody can reject you as a person, and even though you were together on a few dates and spent some time together, that doesn't imply he knows all about you and refuses you as a person. He is merely rejecting a situation; respect that. Interestingly, it does not imply that no one will ever want to date you again. Remember that at some point, you will find yourself on the other side of the coin. Remember when you rejected a person who was crushing on you because you didn't find him compatible or at that time you were surprised by your friend's confession of his emotional love for you when all you could see is a good friend? At this point, you understood that it was better for both of you not to date. Understanding why you made that decision may help stop you from taking it personally when someone rejects you.

"If you have never rejected someone before, believe, you meet a lot of people who just don't seem compatible with you, and then you appreciate how well they respect your decision. You will want to imagine if they all have stayed dejected and formed a lesser opinion of themselves; if they had all felt inferior and buried in the shadows of low self-esteem. But realizing that it is not like, will make you understand there a certain level of emotional maturity is needed when you can emerge from a rejection."

The greatest enemy to self-esteem is the thoughts about the possible cause of rejection. You begin to wonder if you lack something other women have, you begin to make wrong analogies, you begin to have an inflated image of the guy, seeing yourself as not worthy of his standards. The problem is that this might make you settle for less, you may end up loving a guy who might not be your dream man, you may begin to lower the standards of your choices in guys, and this would eventually backfire as you would never get the kind of true love you deserve. People prefer to embrace this paralyzing idea and entertain it in their minds for whatever reason. However, do not allow the mentality to rule over you. Like a toilet paper caught in your shoe; do not let it follow you. You need to stay shoulder high, don't think of yourself as a stupid person, just because you experience all this, appreciate the value of yourself, keep hoping for your dream partner, in life, great things come to those who can accept themselves and never settle for less.

Another factor that may affect your esteem is scrolling through your crush's or ex's social media pages; understand that it may likely only allow your feelings of disappointment to fester. Also, obsessively keeping tabs on their social media or comparing yourself with the new lady in all of their recent posts may affect your self-worth. You may start seeing things that make you believe you've found the reason why they rejected you; the new girl he posts is taller, she seems smarter, or dresses more exotic, which may all be false; you may not know what you are seeing. For instance, in a post of himself and his newfound love looking elegant at a concert, you will never see the messy argument they had before leaving home.

Social media is a big scam; people don't post their worst; everyone appears happy online. If you find it difficult letting their social media pages be, you can start following what is going up with the like you used to. You may de-friend or block him on social media, or at least hide his posts. Delete him from your phone, so you aren't tempted to re-initiate contact through calls or chat. If you want to stop thinking about him constantly and ensure that you do not make it any harder to move on, you need to stop the cyber-stalking. Particularly, in the beginning, it is very likely you feel desperate to contact the guy, and your willpower may only be enough to get you past this urge when you're sober; this may tempt you to give alcohol a trial, but it'll only worsen the situation because alcohol impairs judgment. One of your biggest blunders is to look for someone to blame for it when you feel unrequited love. You can neither blame him nor blame yourself. It just makes you feel worse. You may easily see yourself and discover defects, which might lead you to place irrelevant blame on yourself.

Affirmations might be helpful in reminding oneself that you are not to blame. You might say something like, "I am deserving of love," or "It was not my fault." Instead of alcohol, try ordinary juice or wine and avoid negativity. You may overcome negative thoughts by grooming positive ones. Amy Chan, an expert relationship coach, suggests that you remind yourself that the idea of a one-and-only soul mate is a myth. There are many people out there you could be compatible with.

- ## **Be easy on yourself and forgive yours**

- ## ***elf**

Forgiveness is usually described as an intentional decision to renounce wrath, resentment, and revenge. However, while you can be kind to forgive others, you might have much more difficulty forgiving yourself. It's essential to understand how to learn from mistakes of this kind, allow yourself to be forgiven. You may begin to blame yourself, asking yourself why you fell in love with him in the first place. Self-forgiveness doesn't mean you let yourself be free from concern for your action, and it isn't a sign of weakness neither. Whether you forgive yourself or someone else who wrongs you, the act of forgiveness does not mean that you accept the conduct as being right. Forgiveness implies accepting the actions, accepting what has happened, and being ready to go beyond them and live your life without contemplating events that cannot be reversed.

There are four Rs of self-forgiveness which you need to take note of. The first R is the responsibility, accept responsibility for what has happened, even though it wasn't your fault, yet it is your life at stake. The first step towards self-forgiveness is to confront what you did or what happened. It's the most difficult. If you create excuses, rationalize or explain your acts to make them appear acceptable, the farther you would be running from forgiving yourself. You might think you are doing yourself a favor through rationalizing, but you may be doing the exact opposite.

The second R is to remorse, and you must be careful to draw a line between remorse and self-blame. Remorse comes only if you can identify a fault of yours in the whole escaped; if not, and yet you criticize yourself about what transpired, it is then self-blame and not remorse.

The third R is for repair. If you truly identify your fault, try to take steps as may be necessary to mend the damage; if you have no fault, you have nothing to repair, so let your heart be at peace knowing that you've done no wrong.

The final R is a renewal, and this is a pledge made to yourself never to repeat any action that has contributed to your fault in the current issue. You may feel angry at yourself and begin to engage in self-condemnation; oh –no, nothing is wrong with you, all you've been through is completely normal, you've got it right, falling in love or crushing on a guy is not a wrong idea, expressing your love and desire for him is not a bad idea, telling him your true feelings, expressing your heart is evidence of emotional maturity, you don't need to blame yourself, just forgive yourself.

Honestly, you may feel like you've done yourself some harm; you start wishing you never met him or never caught feelings for him. Remember that all these were beyond your control; emotional attraction is most often not our artificial creation; why should you blame yourself for something in the order of nature? We are created to love, and we can't bottle this emotion; it may cause more harm than you think when you refuse to express your true love. You need to encourage yourself; you're still your beautiful self, there are still millions of people in the universe who can appreciate your true worth.

That awful feeling that comes with rejection often takes a while, and the process of forgiving yourself is so gradual that you might not realize the progress you're making as it happens. That's why it's recommended to recognize milestones of feeling better, especially when you realize that you're starting to move on from him altogether. Start by watching how you spent every day closely. If you are able to spend a day without blaming yourself, that's a huge milestone, and you should acknowledge it accordingly.

There is a need to ensure that your happiness isn't relying on someone's approval. Sure, the guy didn't respond to your affections as you hoped for. He could probably have made things worse by teasing you flirtingly, toying with your emotions, knowing well your true feelings; in all, the primary person responsible for making you happy should be you. Happiness at this point should be a matter of personal choice, and you should take charge of your life and pull yourself out of the misery this situation might have put you.

Some experts suggest that you make a list of things you do on your own and major ways in which you stay independent. For instance, you might be financially independent. If you're in a school, you may be a lone wolf reader who can pass on her own, consider these ways by which you take charge of your happiness; this will make it easy for you not to blame yourself since you can even achieve those things without his input. It may help bring a feeling of calmness and settle the friction that you might be raising against yourself deep down. Remember that this is not the end of the role but a process, and it will get better

Eventually, you're going to feel good enough about your sense of judgment. Realize that you are better off. It doesn't matter how great the guy is; if he doesn't love you, you could not be happy with him. It's very easy to forgive yourself, especially if you have invested a lot of energy falling in love with them. Stepping back to accept reality without being cruel or judgmental can help you get to heal. It is ok to feel bad about the person for not seeing enough reason to be with you without blaming that person. Don't let your friends play it either. Your friends may try to abuse him verbally for not loving you. Tell them that "it isn't fair to blame him for something he can't help; let's focus on me getting over him."

Case II: Dealing with a cheating boyfriend
I know sometimes it is just too hard to deal with heartbreak. So, you really want to suck it all up and be dealing with pain? Well, I won't let you do that. Why keep hurting so bad when you can actually move on, you've got the power and the strength to do so. I know it is hard, like really hard, and you do not want to deal with it now or later. So, you start making up excuses for him and yourself. Do you really think that is going to help? Hell no.

When communication fails to change a cheating guy, you may feel devastated, like air got snuffed out of you; you won't believe the man you were so loyal to is the same man who now cares so less about you. You have already given all you could to the relationship, but it didn't work out due to his immoral nature, and the chance is high that you might want to blame yourself for his action, for instance, you may start thinking within yourself; what if I had spent more time with him, If only I allow us to have sex more regularly, I wish I had firmer boobs or bigger ass, he wouldn't have cheated, If only I had been sexier, The girl he cheated on me with seems curvy than me.

The fact is you didn't push him to cheat, and you wouldn't be able to pull him from cheating, a lot of thoughts and emotions will overwhelm you, but you need to relax and not give way for these thoughts to cloud your life. You shouldn't also blame the other woman or women he sleeps with. In some cases, your ex could have told her that he has no woman in his life. When your ex cheated with her, it wasn't because she dressed to kill or seduced him; she has nothing you don't already possess. A cheating ex is a cheater, the work of a cheater is to cheat, and he doesn't need any excuse. If you've nursed any anger towards the women he cheated with, please forgive and focus on the guy who promised you heaven and earth.

• **Will he stop cheating?**

I have understood that a cheating boyfriend mostly does not quit; that is the apparent truth because it is not the woman, and it is definitely not you. If you take out the picture of the woman he cheated with, you'll see that there are millions of women that could replace her as your ex's cheat mate, so the problem was all about him; the fault belongs to him, and no one else is to blame.

Cheating is a pattern of behavior that doesn't easily detach from its victim; cheaters cheat and cheat all over again till they stop feeling remorseful. The first thing is to make peace with yourself, which is a tough thing to do when you're feeling hurt. Making peace with yourself is not accepting that his action was fine, but it will not deny you joy. You have no power over his actions, but you can manage your reaction to them. Remember that people and things can vanish, but you have a peace that no one can take from you when you are happy with yourself.

• **Reasons you need to move on?**

One bitter truth is that, after communication has failed to change a cheating partner, you may not be able to get over him till you leave him. However, you've given it your best; you gave him trust; he betrayed it. You gave him a new chance, and he spoilt it. You took your time to communicate it with him; he forfeited that chance. You waited it out, you kept hopes high, you didn't cheat back, you didn't get mad or abusive, what else could you do? All you have to do now is to strengthened yourself, concentrate your efforts on you now. He is genuinely an ingrate who doesn't deserve a good heart like yours and the world doesn't revolve around him, so move on, refresh your view, and you'll be amazed where it can land you at. You need to understand that he has taken you for granted

In my experience, I have realized that only a few things can puncture your confidence like infidelity does, mainly because you might be figuring that he did it because you have specific inadequacies. To deal with a cheater's aftermath, most people seek professional help by consulting therapists. If you think you need it, please do not hesitate. You deserve some peace after all you've been through; you can't be a slave to his manipulation forever. Not only does this worth your effort, but you are also worth the effort, and you are a good and valuable person who deserves to be treated well with respect and decency.

Cheating and being loyal are both self-made decisions. He has no right more than you do in the relationship. So why does he keep cheating? Believe it or not, nothing can justify it because if you also want to cheat on him, you could have done so, but you choose to stay disciplined.

Therefore, He has no excuse, and clearly has no conscience and doesn't care about or for you or your feelings, he is only using you, and you must not tolerate this, leaving him will be difficult because you love him, but you must be determined to leave this toxic relationship. Just like you decided to stay faithful to him, you are strong enough to make any decision and stand by it. Rebuilding life without him can seem distressing initially, but you will find it exciting and peaceful with time. You won't need to worry about who he might be cheating with again, and you won't need to hold out hope of a changed partner to only discover he is the same old dog eating the same old vomit, getting your heart broken over and over again. People like this don't deserve space in your heart. Format him from your inner heart; peace cannot be brought by talking to him again. Peace wouldn't come naturally in this scenario; you need to create stability for yourself.

Another thing you should know is that when he abandoned you wherever you were and go on cheating with other ladies, he feels they make him happier, understands him better, cares for him more. So, he will try to reciprocate it to them. Believe me, he would have spent more time, money, and attention on them than you within that period. If he loves you, he wouldn't have gone that far.

There is a general saying that when people show you their actual color, believe them. Cheaters always cheat; it is not connected with boredom. It is only a moral flaw that can make someone break solemn promises made to you. The fact that he broke this one can even be a red flag that he's bound to break more in the future, not just your sexual sanctity vow but some other promise he might have made to you. This guy will only stop you from seeing one of the good men out there; you do not need to doubt it. Even if you try harder after communication has failed to make him change, you need to know that the relationship cannot return to how it used to be. You will always have reason to question his social media chats, telephone conversations, his whereabouts, and female work partners because a part of you will always doubt his faithfulness. The truth is that once you see someone with a greater sense of loyalty, you begin to wonder what attracted you to him in the first place.

Now is time for you to think of the millions of other people around the world who have passed through the same thing you're experiencing currently at one point or another, think about what happened to them, think about the feelings you have right now; they felt precisely the same way. Although some of them felt worse than you, our response to grief is different. So, some of them start feeling better after a day; some take a week or weeks, while others may take up to months before the healing process begins. The majority only start feeling better after a year or couple of years.

But the truth is when you later remember these things, it will feel like it never happened before. In 10 years, you struggle to remember the guy's name. After 20 years, it becomes a mere memory, and after 30 years, you may even laugh when you remember it. It will only come as a flash; a quick glimpse of the whole escapade may flash in your mind like lightning, having absolutely zero impact on you. So far, this is the normal process of pain and healing, and it will begin as soon as you give it a chance. It is called "time." So, give time a chance; believe me, you're going to be fine; it'll all be history. It will help if you allow time to meditate upon things you can do to help you further down the healing road. This should be your motivation, strive towards self-fulfillment. What are other things that make you feel great, outline them and focus on them; by doing this, you are giving time the needed opportunity to help heal your broken spirit.

You also need to prevent his cheating habit from jeopardizing your level of trust. Dealing with a guy that keeps cheating will make you stop trusting people. In fact, it will make you see the whole world as a lie. This is a terrible state of mind for your personal progress and happiness.

Surprisingly, we live in a world where we depend on each other to survive. No matter how much the distance is between two people, they've got to sometimes meet and trust each other without a reasonable level of proof. This is humanity. Dealing with someone who keeps making you look stupid and taking your trust for granted will affect your interpersonal relationship with others who do not deserve your doubt.

Please resist the temptation to get stuck in your past emotions for him. He's not worth your teardrop, so you don't need to cry for him; spending time in the thoughts of a man who treated you like dirt is a complete waste of your time. You are worthy of a man who can appreciate your value and beauty, not just the beauty of your body, the firmness of your breast, or the curves of your ass, but someone who can see your inner beauty, the beauty of your heart, someone who appreciates value inside-out. You need someone who can treat you to the same standard of trust, like a princess, spending beautiful moments of mutual understanding and zero interest in cheating. But, as they always say, all good and bad things must come to an end, the good moments you had with him should not be a reason why you keep up with his new provocations, you shouldn't bear with such attitudes, because you risk your good spirit getting crush by the burden of his persistent unfaithfulness.

Keep yourself motivated and protected from his negative energy; you need to preserve your positive energy. No matter how attached you feel, a cheat is not a good person for you nor for anyone else for that matter. The worse of all is that if you don't let go of him at this stage, his friend will mock you, whenever they are alone, he'll tell them jokingly how you forgave him when he cheated, how you communicate with him over it and how he shuns your words, they will all turn you to laughing stock. If you decided to cling to him, expect more hurt, disrespect, emotional abuse, and mental torture. Staying with a cheat is a sure guarantee of sadness.

Knowing that you do not have a future with him or at least a happy future with him is also enough reason to move on. If you refuse to focus on yourself right now, and you keep thinking about him, you might regret it in the future. Even if you end up together, you will eventually hate him and hate yourself. You should also remember that plenty of good guys are looking for loyal girlfriends, so why not dumb his ass in the nearest dust bin. I think he even gave you a clear answer; the relationship is over, his loyalty has shifted, and men don't find it attractive when you beg them to stay. So let him know you stand by your values

You need to pay more attention to other things that make you happy, or you will find it almost impossible to focus on your self-development. For instance, join a local tennis club where you meet and relate with other people if you like tennis. Your time within this group will be a great chance to carry your thoughts away from the guy who just caused you great pains and rejected you.

- ## Avoid the intention to get back at him

When you think moving on is impossible, it is likely to want to get revenge too. However, this is not always a reasonable thing to do. In a bid to get revenge, you might be tempted to do the same thing he did to you in order to hurt him back. Some people advise that you can revenge by having sex with his best friends, this will only make folly of you, the wise saying that birds of the same feather flock together is very accurate, his friends are likely people of the same mind, in fact, if not they should be one of the people that rebuke him for his actions and genuinely seek to bring you guys together. Don't ever fall into this trap. It will make a mockery of the values you stand for and make them see you as a potential cheat who never got the chance to cheat. It will be a cause for celebration in their camp while you continue to reel in regret.

So, understand that you should realize that you are smarter and far matured than that. You can't afford to give yourself cheaply to some guys because you want to get back at the guy. Any guy who would get in bed with you should offer more than a free ride into your body because you are angry with someone. Don't worry about revenge because he will realize the value of what he lost in due time. He will remember your sweat, pain, and tears and wonder how he managed to hurt such a beautiful soul as you.

- ## You do not need revenge; you just need to move on

Until we discuss how to move on from heartbreak, keep in mind that just that you've been cheated upon doesn't mean you'll always be cheated on; the truth is that not all men cheat. Even though some people will hastily generalize that all men cheat, it is a wrong notion. There are very good men with a golden heart that will never intentionally hurt your feelings. Your recent experience can make you think that they are rare to find, but they do exist. But you have to give it time, don't rush any man, let them see the actual value in you and come for you, and when they do, take things slowly.

- ## Use your previous experience wisely

Though you may find it impossible to tell when a guy will cheat, and it is not your responsibility to stalk him or prevent him from cheating. However, previous experience with a cheater can expose you to similar things among guys who cheat. This can help you prevent unnecessary heartbreak. The truth is that cheaters are not always perfect lairs; once you notice sharp inconsistencies that can be a potential cheating partner. For instance, try to see if they keep to time and schedules, or they always find an excuse for why you wouldn't meet again at the last minute. If it becomes rampant that they seem not to keep to time and plans you make together, it is a red flag you should try to investigate closely. Also, watch for inconsistency in communications.

Cheating is about secrecy, and cheaters may intentionally keep their cells unavailable without battery or signal issues to keep the original and cheat mates from possibly gaining insights about each other. A sharp change in phone use habits may also be a sign you should avoid a potential partner. For instance, if they change the access code without telling you or lock apps with unique passwords or app lock, watch out if they stop picking calls in your front or always clear the SMS inbox area. If a potential partner also becomes less around without any probable cause, it might be a sign that there is someone that's demanding more time from them

Another thing to watch out for is their faithfulness to financial obligations. If they seem to miss some financial obligation, is it due to being poor, alcoholism, or an unknown factor? Such unknown factors could signify a womanizing partner, so be careful not to fall into the same hands again. You should also look out if there's a woman they speak intimately with but which they never told you about; who knows, he might be married or committed to someone else; all these will save you from potentially infidel partners.

You should also look out whether his schedules change without any reasonable excuse. For instance, someone who gets back from work quite early but started coming back late, without any apparent changes in their work schedule, looks out whether they are also periodically unavailable without any definite cause.

Another sign you need to look out for is if they stop telling you details of how they spent their day, or their narrative doesn't add up, they could probably be sharing more with the new chick and unintentionally shifting focus from you. Still, you need to be very smart to recognize these instances. Another funny but true attribute of some cheaters is that they may start giving you more gift than usual, by so doing, they seek to make you not focus attention on other red flags that shows from their action, watch out for excess or unnecessary gift, or gifts that are ridiculously expensive on a basis more regular than usual.

Finally, to avoid the same pitfall, when you notice any of the above attributes in a potential new partner and you summon the courage to ask them about it, watch out if they suddenly become defensive and outburst hot emotions. They knew what you already went through with the previous guy and are determined to make themselves look like a dove that would never hurt in other to keep you at all costs. If they are innocent, they won't probably get unnecessarily defensive.

STAGE 4

Cutting ties

"

From the time you broke up, it is possible that you have been contacting your partner or crush frequently. He might want to be friendly about this and even leave comments on all your social media posting. If you two meet coincidentally, he may want to appear a little uplifting just make sure you are comfortable.

However, after devoting your time and energy to loving a person, as well as having an open dialogue and expression of your emotions for him, if he declines your proposal, the next significant step is to break all relations with him. From my experience, this is one of the most challenging decisions to make in life. But I want you to understand that cutting connections with him is better for your physical, mental, and emotional health regardless of how tough it is. The very decision not to try any harder, the thoughts of the time, resources, and dedication you've given him, all these may be pulling you down. However, if you want these steps to be helpful, you need to be brave, and you need a lot of self-confidence.

Once you ascertain that your boyfriend or crush isn't ready to reciprocate your love, it is advisable to end it as soon as possible. The more you delay this, the more miserable you are bound to feel. Don't wear yourself out trying to persuade your crush to alter their viewpoint or trying to impress your boyfriend to see enough reasons to continue with you. Push relationships may be like trying to squeeze into a pair of too tiny shoes. They will not work, no matter how much you like them. It really doesn't mean those shoes aren't good; it all just means they're not the correct pair for you in that situation. No one should feel obligated to be in a relationship or compelled to date someone. If you intend to take such steps, both of you should be equally enthused about it rather than being pressured into it. What you have to do at this point is to cut ties and connections that can trigger unnecessary memory of them. Your love expressed to a guy would be returned in an ideal world, but life isn't a fantasy. It is very natural to experience "sadness" whenever the subject of your passion does not share your feelings. Pay attention to yourself as you deal with your frustration. One of the main reasons why you need to cut ties is that you must not allow rejection to get hold of your future. As stated earlier, it is a part of life, but it's a part one must move on from; nobody deserves to get trapped in a state of heartbroken.

The more reason why it's really hard to cut ties this day and age is that there's rarely privacy; we all could easily bump into each other, especially over the internet. Or how do you cut ties with a person when the internet can afford a myriad of cold means of stalking? It all begins with your inherent resolve, strong will, and determination. Achieving physical and emotional cuts requires you to be strong. Thoughts of this guy you're trying to cut will cross your mind; you need to be ready for some emotional struggle.

• **Cut intimate communication**

Stopping intimate communication with someone when it may negatively impact you is a liberating move. What is envisaged here is cutting intimate communication; this happens when you can't afford to cut all communications. For instance, you might be classmates or partners in a joint project where talking to them is unavoidable. It's time to stop all the emotional and more profound aspects of your communication. The first step is that if you're comfortable doing so, tell them about your new limits. Although this may appear contradictory, it is the most direct approach to expressing your thoughts to them and helps avoid misinterpretation. Explain to the individual that continuing the intimate talks you used to have might be causing you problems. You'd be taking actions to put significant distance to such forms of discussions; if the guy is mature and understanding enough, he would be supportive of your cautious approach. You could say, for instance, "I respect your decision and understand we can't have a relationship; I wouldn't love us to continue having those intimate talks again, to avoid unnecessary feelings, So I've chosen to give myself some breathing room over the next few months. During that period, I will not be replying to any social media messages." Ensure that your mode of talking to him remains firm but in a kind manner.

Avoid speaking to them aggressively; neither should you speak passively; the emphasis must be on assertiveness. If you prefer not to speak with them in person, write them a letter. It may be tough to speak properly if you feel intimidated or anxious around the individual. In this situation, write them a letter detailing your feelings and explaining that you will no longer be communicating with them. However, speaking to them in person offers some advantages; it shows you're emerging quickly past your pains and bracing your storm, while the letter option also does not show less of you. If you wouldn't like to see them, send the letter to his home. Intimacy is a process, and cutting intimate communication with someone is also procedural, you must avoid unnecessary solicitation and communication with them, you must understand that not only words can breed intimate communications, at times, but action also speaks louder than voice, you don't need to reach out to them for help if you can avoid it if you can't, there's no harm in trying, just make sure you keep your business with them really short and simple. Are you sick? You may talk to some other friend, relative, or colleague about it. Do you need help fixing something? Why not talk to someone else and avoid building unnecessary friction between you again! Whenever and wherever possible, avoid the individual. This gives you some breathing room as you recover from the tough or toxic connection.

This isn't always easy, so try to avoid them wherever possible. Consider going to a new coffee shop if the individual consistently goes to the same coffee shop. If you live with the individual, you should consider finding another place to reside. At this point, you may need to adopt the no contact rule, avoid texting, phoning, or messaging them, and try to reduce contact in any manner you can. This involves avoiding areas you know they frequent, such as their favorite restaurant or coffee shop. While you may believe you want to see or speak to them afterward, all you are doing is satisfying perverse desires and hurting yourself. Consider designating a buddy as an intermediary if you really must contact this individual for financial, logistical, or some other kind of concerns. If this individual needs to send you a message, they may do so through your buddy and vice versa. Pretend you're on the phone if he approaches you for social interaction; pretend to be on a call or texting. Pretending to be in the middle of a discussion with someone else will discourage him from participating in the conversation without appearing impolite. Believe me, and he wouldn't like to look unnecessarily intrusive. Imitate the phone conversation or text message as closely as possible. Avoid making eye contact, walk back and forth, or immediately inform him that you are on a critical call or need to complete an essential text. If you find yourself trapped in the middle of an unpleasant or embarrassing conversation with him, respectfully excuse yourself and go out. Give some excuse. Create a variety of factors such that you may quickly divert a talk before it begins. This is especially necessary if he stops or approaches you unexpectedly. Telling him you have to rush to board a bus is an excellent and convincing reason. Other reasons, such as being late for another appointment or forgetting something at the office, are great but must be accompanied by a feeling of urgency. Enroll friends' support; for instance, you may have a buddy phone or send an SMS that demands immediate reaction if you find yourselves in an unavoidable social scenario with him. Explain that you have overlapping plans if he asks you to a social gathering.

All these will deny him the needed chance to ignite intimate talks with you again. To avoid establishing a conversation that might raise closeness again, you can also open a book, magazine, or newspaper and start reading. You can carry a book or magazine in your luggage, whether sitting alone or on public transit. It will help you appear busy and unready for conversation, yet you'll not be merely wasting your time but learning from the material you're holding. Whether or not the earbuds are plugged in, use a headset or earpiece. To persuade the guy, the plug should be kept out of sight and not necessarily attached. Using an earphone in public gives you the image of being unapproachable and busy. It is one of the most considerate ways to express your unavailability.

Appear to be busy or preoccupied with a task. It is not always feasible to avoid interacting with others, particularly in school or the workplace. Act being completely interested in a product or email so that people would feel awkward interrupting you. Use your laptop to type. Launch an existing document or correspondence to give the impression that you are deep in contemplation. Find items in your workspace to keep you occupied. Filing paperwork and generating duplicates are two basic methods to appear preoccupied. When you are addressed despite looking too busy, merely accept their comments and withdraw yourself nicely to carry on working. Whispering or mumbling to yourself while working frequently indicates that you are deep in concentration and will discourage him from bothering you. Excuse yourself respectfully by claiming you have quite a great deal of work to accomplish or that you'll have to get back to your workspace.

Write an email or text message if the person is an associate with whom you must maintain regular contact for official objectives. Instead of contacting him, write him an email. He might be your boss, instructor, or coworker. Keep in mind that such an email can let you retain a considerable distance without causing unnecessary stress in a formal setting. You may also send a brief text message instead of speaking. Text messages may be beneficial in ensuring contact without appearing harsh or aloof. You might have already sent 70% of the information you need to pass over text, and this helps you keep the time spent in contact with them short and simple.

- **Avoid them on social media**

In the words of Ami Angelowicz, rightly stated that "Social media is like a funhouse. It warps everything, makes it giant or small or headless, unrecognizable, most notably, your sense of self and reality. It takes your imagination on a wild tilt-a-whirl of imagined scenarios and possibilities. It's a warped mirror, reflecting your worst fears and deepest insecurities. We certainly understand how appealing it is to go through a crush's social media pages, but doing so would most certainly exacerbate your emotions of rejection.

Numerous studies and research demonstrate that continuing to observe your unrequited guy lover over social networks will simply prolong your pain. It is so easy to do, though; it takes real determination to resist the urge. We seem unable to help the thirst. In fact, we are hooked to the anguish of wanting to see him or to see the new lady he's going out with. You might want to examine what ways she seems better than you. You must understand that ignoring somebody in social media may be difficult, especially when that person you are trying to avoid cannot stop running into you, or if they are attempting to chat with you and pretend not to understand you're avoiding him. Remove his contact details. Go on and delete his mobile number so that you won't be bothered to text or call it. Don't ever contact him on social media; resist the urge because naturally, it may come. This will quicken your healing process and ensure there's no fear of your heart getting broken by him again when you see him post the photo of another lady. Keep in mind to also erase his emails, voice notes, and texts to prevent you from going back and reading or listening to them.

Quit monitoring his Facebook, Twitter, blog, Pinterest, and every other social network related to his account. Do not spend every waking moment of the day glancing or scanning at his social networking fields. Besides being unhealthy, you can do a lot more fascinating things than refreshing his Instagram, Facebook, or Twitter page. Pokenosing into how he is faring at such a period will simply make life tougher for you. Unfollow or unfriend him if you cannot withstand the temptation of stalking his social media field. While being friends or followers, if he has ever provided you with passwords, politely urge him to reset his passcode to prevent the temptation to spy or stalk on him.

Consider blocking them: Some people consider banning individuals on social media to be petty, but I see it as a kind of self-care. Consider this. What would you do if a TV show is broadcasting content that you wouldn't want to watch? Sit around and put up with that because you think it's nice to the actors? No. You switch the channel.

Similarly, instead of exposing yourself to information that may be detrimental to your emotional well-being on media platforms, you should do the same. When a user is blocked, they are virtually erased from existence. Consider the following benefits of blocking him: You cannot view his profiles or search for his names. His images, videos, and status updates are no longer visible in your feeds. You can no longer be tag him in your post, neither can he tag you on his own.

o Facebook:

You may utilize the Mute option in Facebook Messenger if you still want to remain friends with him for some reason but wouldn't want any messages from him. You may block him if this is not sufficient so that your Facebook relationship is ended and no direct interaction from both sides is allowed. You may use the block option: by clicking on the menu button (3 horizontal points) on his user's profile or via the Messenger chat menu or the general Facebook site.

o Instagram and Twitter:

On Twitter, you must follow him before he sends you a direct message unless you open the DMs to everyone by default, so by unfollowing him, you can easily block his messages. As for when he mentions you in your timeline, you may conceal it by muting (on any profile page, click on the cog symbol) (again via the same cog icon or the expanded menu that appears by his tweet). In his Instagram chat threads, you may discover identical mute and block choices (touch the i-icon for the blocking setup).

Now that you have successfully blocked the guy on your social media networks, you can go about your business without fear of seeing their terrible posts in your feeds, and this will bring unprecedented relief to your mental and emotional health.

- **Throw away unwanted souvenirs from your relationship/ Emails/ Gifts/Jewelry**

Remove from your vicinity things that could serve as reminders. Are you with a picture you snapped with him? Do you still have it hung on your wall, or probably kept somewhere in your room? Remove or put it away. Do you have an old sweater or clothe of them in your wardrobe? Give it out or burn it off. It may make it difficult to get his thought off your mind.

These small reminders can do significant damages to your mental and emotional life. This should be extended to electronics reminders you may have of them, videos you took together, pictures of your vacation, or voice note records should all be deleted from your device. If you've been around each other for a period, you probably have certain things which you see and triggers his image in your mental faculty.

If you have in possession any personal material that could be valuable, maybe certificates, documents, or jewelry, put it in a box and mail it back to him, or leave it on his front step. Try to avoid physical contact while returning his kinds of stuff, and this also includes anything that he may have specifically kept in your hand. Another approach to view things is this. If you get caught on a red light, and it turns green all of a sudden, everyone there moves forward, and you're just trapped. You'll be punished for loitering in the middle of the road or being struck by yet another vehicle. You may move, but your foot has to be pressed on the pedal. Get going. You don't want to be stranded anymore in the red signal. Remove his picture if you've posted it on your social network before; the more you view it, the more you are tempted to contact him. You may find a buddy to deliver it to avoid meeting him entirely.

You must be careful not to destroy his things, remember it might not be a good idea to smoke all their objects by burning them in a bonfire. Instead of destruction, try hard to return them or give them out. Remove clothing, letters, and presents he sent to you. If you are not sure you're willing to let go of it, store everything in a carton. Delete the emails he sent you. If you believe that some conversations may be essential for the future, make a folder, insert every correspondence, and plan to revise it at a future date. If they have anything belonging to you that you might need, do not hesitate to request it from them; if you leave it in his hands, the thought of it will indirectly remind you of him and a host of unpleasant memories, to avoid physical contact you can have them mail it to you or ask a friend to get it for you. If they decline to return it in a gentlemanly manner, try to forget it if you can afford it, and if not, you need to exercise patience then ask after a while. Hopefully, he should be reasonable enough to return it without creating unnecessary drama. If he chooses not to return it, you may consider involving appropriate third parties such as his friends or if you have mutual friends, tell them to get it for you, if all other options fail, kindly ignore such property, it shows the kind of guy you were dying to be with.

- **Do what you do together with someone more fun**

Allowing your boyfriend or crush to go doesn't imply that your friends and relatives can't offer affection. Take a couple of weeks to interact with them every week just to cruise around. Gist with them and have limitless fun. Please spend much time with people you love and care about. Invite some pals to hang around and watch Netflix if you don't like doing anything. Isolating yourself is likely to make you feel terrible, so leaning on your network of friends is vital. Members of your family can also aid. Take counsel and consolation from your parents or your relatives or anybody else.

You do not need to remember the same activities you enjoyed doing with him. But if you remember doing things like going on mountaineering together or you visit nature parks, do the same together with your inner circle of friends. Get together for dinner, watch a film, and arrange a trip or spa. Try out fun activities with friends. And whether you're with pals or alone, try some fun activities, something you always wanted to test. You can bring a companion or two if you have difficulties getting your thoughts off things. They can assist you in diverting your thinking so that you can have memorable moments together. It's difficult to do away with your affection for a guy, but you can do it with a bit of support from friends and family. Call a buddy to speak instead of withdrawing alone.

You should not often be disturbed by the rejection of the proposal. When you feel like talking, the guy must have been one of your most crucial talk mates for the past few periods, but you can now call on another friend or group of friends, share your mind with them, request their opinion, and never be afraid to spill your inner thoughts. Consider the things that make you feel comfortable, including shopping in the company of friends or going to get a new hairstyle. Go through with it to get the man out of your head. Give yourself a fresh appearance, purchase something new, take the week off and just hear your favorite songs while singing along with friends. It may all help you unstressed and refocus on anything but him. If you've got time and resources, try traveling somewhere overnight. It must not be far away—it can only imply remaining in the house of a friend. It will pull you off your comfort zone, and this is where you are most likely to keep thinking of the guy you should be getting over.

Reconnect with old friends or create new pals. If the guy belongs in your circle of friends or is close to someone you are very close to, it's essential to broaden your social network. There are good friends you may unintentionally have abandoned during the heat of your passion for the guy, don't be afraid to pick your phone and call them. Ask whether they would love to hang out. Recommend to them to visit the cinema. If they recommend some other suitable venue or activity to you, give it a trial, be flexible to their opinion, and allow rebounding like old times. Focusing on the guy has limited your scope for a while; now, you're like a bird released from the bars, fly wide, fly high. Look beyond the horizon in the company of people who matter.

At the heat of your crush on the guy, it could have seemed no one else exists, but now that you realize the value of your network in a new term, utilize it to the fullest. No matter the temptation or urge, don't separate or isolate yourself from your loved ones. Be sure you enjoy yourselves, and it is good to take a while to appreciate and reconnect with your friends; whatever your relationship status is, they can never deny you.

There is a natural tendency to attempt to keep pain within. This tendency grows out of feeling horrible about something. This is still a reaction that will delay your healing process. Probably it is because you're ashamed of being denied or because you don't wish to get others to share in your pain, or just because you don't feel comfortable revealing your vulnerability. Those who care about you and want you to feel more comfortable would never be happy if you are passing through bad feelings. Have a rethink if you are reluctant to trouble your friends with it. These are your pals; they owe a duty to make you feel better and aid you. It'll give you a great sense of relief when you share with them the burdens of your heart. Plan dinner, visit the mall and go on a shopping spree. Laughing generates endorphins which is the hormone of happiness; it makes you feel joyful and healthy.

Spend time and enjoy doing things you love with individuals who make you cheerful. Go to a nightclub and giggle while you're trying to scream out pop tunes. Go to a playground or play a sport you enjoy. Watching funny movies or comedy skits may also boost endorphins. Watch a comedy, stream funny clips and hilarious internet videos, or just looking for amusing gifs. Cheerfulness increases resilience to pain. It stimulates the same parts of your brain as physical pain when you feel emotional anguish, so you need extra activities to gladden your temperance. Let them purchase a drink for you and let them remind you of how great you are.

Require help from close friends or family members, especially someone who has experienced a similar thing before. Many individuals can relate to your experience to a certain degree and may share their own crush experience. Nevertheless, they can provide you certain highly skilled advice even though they do not have firsthand knowledge of this subject.

- **Keep physical distance: Avoid revisiting your date spots**

All of your previous places should be avoided? If there are recollections of the spot where you hugged or had your first kiss, remain away from going there. Though these experiences can't escape your memory, no need to build old recollections that complicate this procedure. Out of sight is out of mind; make sure you keep yourself busy enough that you won't have a chance to make time for physical contact with them. If you share similar hobbies that might make you come across, for instance, if you use the same public gym, try to find another gym. This might be impossible if you are classmates or co-workers; you both need to report in class or at the workplace as the case may be what you do is limit your physical contact in such a situation to the barest minimum. For instance, don't go if he works in the mall and your buddies want to go there. Stay at home and do another thing.

The primary purpose is to keep going, and most individuals in love will come back to previous sentiments as soon as they see their beloved one again or as soon as they begin to interact with it. So be sure you're not going to see them. It would help if you also tried to avoid spots you've both been together; there are two reasons for this; the first one is that it might be his favorite spots and you run the risk of running into him unintended; the second risk is that each time you go there, it will trigger a memory of the times you had together, which might affect your focus from your healing process to ruminating on frivolities. You may attend the same church; if they have a favorite spot in church, try to avoid sitting there for now; as we progress, you will see when you can start to maintain physical contact, but for now, strict physical distance is advised if it is possible.

Apart from the fact that maintaining physical distance can trigger memories, it may also trigger emotions. For instance, if you avoid physical distance, you wouldn't need to meet his new love, not to talk of getting trapped in awkward eye contact. All these contribute indirectly to your healing process, and the truth is that the fact that you love them and have been in constant physical distance recently will make it difficult for you to avoid this contact. You've strolled the street together, go shopping together, and took the same taxi or Uber; doing this thing alone now will make you want to miss them; you must therefore resist this urge. If they specifically call you for a hookup, it is advisable to decline. Out of optimism, you might think he probably had a rethink, but if it turns out he's merely interested in watching your pain, it would only add salt to your injury.

Note that cutting ties is no easy job; it will hurt almost more painful than the initial rejection; it is the ultimate test of your emotional intelligence; the better you fare at this, the easier your whole healing process becomes. In case it appears difficult to concentrate on other things after cutting ties, you may consult a dating expert or psychologist. You should note the complimentary aspects of cutting ties; for instance, if you cut intimate communication, you must seek refuge in another friend, there must be someone else you contact when you have intimate matters to share; this should be either your friends or relatives. You shouldn't just block every user on your social media, and you need to check the posts of others to keep your page lively, comment on other friends' posts, and create your posts to share with friends. It also extends to the case of restricting physical contact, there should be other people you visit or that can accompany you to places you wouldn't love to go alone. In a bit of time, I promise that you'll get used back to being yourself without any shade or impact of the time the guy spent in your life.

STAGE 5

Don't be afraid to be alone/ be independent-minded

"

One hard truth is that the pain of having to deal with a broken relationship, a broken heart, and sometimes unrequited love is what many people have to experience. For you, it may be the first time, and for some people, it may be more than a one-time thing. We will repeatedly meet people who aren't right for us and those who feel we aren't right for them too.

Taking time to heal is hard, but it is a routine we need to understand more. It is like knowing that when you fall, you will rise again. So, no matter how many times you fall and no matter how hard you fall, getting back on your feet is a must, and you deserve that much.

Moving on will cost a lot of energy, so it is ok to take your time before making the decision. However, you do not want to wallow in this situation for too long. If someone you love isn't reciprocating the love, you have every right to live a better life. A broken heart is better than unrequited love.

I know you are scared and you do not want to imagine a life without him in it. Sometimes, we even feel like nothing much is going on for us aside from this love, but you've got to believe that you are worth much more than that because that is the truth. Do not feel like you won't find love again; there is someone somewhere feeling imperfect because you are not there with him, so buckle up your shoes and let get you back on track.

The decision to move on starts from setting your mindset and knowing that you are never alone. You are enough for anyone, and if someone doesn't see that, he is not right for you. Do not be afraid to be alone for some time; that is the period you need to rebuild yourself and see the world differently. Follow the tips below to get yourself together.

- **Try new things**

Moving on is going to give you a lot of time thinking about what would have been if you are together with him. Accept that fact, but you can use this time to think about being a better person. How to be a better version of yourself. Learns new skills and practice is out. Think about what skill you need again. It does not necessarily need to be a skill to make money. You can learn just anything to keep you occupied. This way, you will realize you gradually forget him by not focusing your thought on him.

Trying new things also has a way of making you feel a lot better. For example, gaining new knowledge makes you feel go about how much you learned. Reading new books exposes you to new ideas and fills your imagination with pleasure. New things are not restricted; learn to play the new game, follow the new trend, and try a new style. Just keep your energy on anything that makes you feel good.

• **Exercise**

Set an exercise time that works effectively with your daily schedule. Exercise does more than just keeping you fit; it elevates your soul and empties your mind. Focus more on those exercises that set your mind free. Starting your day with an hour of exercise will refresh your body and mind. It is like breathing in fresh breath. However, this may not be recommended if you are a student or a working-class lady. Suppose this time does not work for you. An hour of exercise in the evening is just as effective as the morning exercise. It will free your mind from sadness or any kind of pain. I will recommend evening exercises like strolling or a steady breathing Yoga technique to free your mind. Set the time for 5:30pm - 7pm

Scientifically, exercise is good for boosting the good vibes and makes you think and see things positively by boosting your body's serotonin and dopamine level. These two neurotransmitters work as mood regulators in the body and make you feel naturally confident. This tends to eliminate depression and pain. It also increases your ability to feel pleasure.

Aside from this evident fact, you already heard that exercise makes you fit and makes you feel a lot refreshed. But this does not end there; staying fit makes you a lot more beautiful, stunning, perfect, and confident.

"While rejection may affect your self-esteem and make you doubt yourself. Exercise will boost your confidence level and make you see yourself in a different light. From firmer skin to a more flexible body, you start to feel entirely different in an excellent way. This will be of great help in mending your heart and can get you back on track quicker than you ever expect."

Ensure that your exercise has a distinct focus when the target is to move on. I recommend trying out exercise that works in progression, this will make you keep doing it regularly, and before you know it, it becomes a hobby that keeps your mind off troubles. So instead of cardio, running can be a good way to start. Focus on running faster or longer. You can also try yoga exercises following videos online. Progress with this by changing the style you practice regularly. The first heartbreak I suffered was a little intense. I really couldn't eat nor sleep for days. I felt unwanted until I pull myself together and hit the gym. Surprisingly, in three days, I was looking for healthy recipes to support my body goal.

• Sleep early

Sleeping early is a way to keep those tedious and painful thoughts out of your mind. You do not need to force it, but you can work towards it. I recalled singing myself a lullaby and listening to the positive affirmation that makes me feel like I have done enough for the day, and that feels good.

Heartbreak may occasion many sleepless nights, but if you do get yourself to bed early, you wake up free-minded like a baby. Start by setting a time to sleep; set it so early and realistic. It will amount to a waste of time if you set an impossible time, probably because of your daily activities.

"If the time is realistic, then it is achievable. One way to get yourself a night of sleep is to listen to lullabies and kids' stories. Find interesting and engaging books that keep you busy during the night, and read it to yourself every night, and before you know it, you are fast asleep already. Another way is to try watching movies, focus on the movie that keeps you distracted but does not render you eager to see the next episode, remember the idea is to fall asleep as early as possible and not stay awake."

I do not recommend boring movies, but something with lessen suspense will be perfect for this purpose. Keep following till you are already feeling dizzy, turn off the TV, and go to bed. Check out movies like "A Charlie Brown Christmas," "Fantastic Planet," and a lot of others.

• Indulge in your favorite hobby

Do not sit down and think during your leisure hours, do something

During heartbreak, making out time to indulge in your hobby may be harder than you think. More than doing something beneficial, you may find yourself mopping around your room and eating those high-fat foods. However, making time out for your hobbies has a lot of benefits for your mental health and can improve your emotional well-being.

I really cannot overemphasize how much goods you will get from indulging in your hobbies during heartbreak. So, if you do not have one, you've got to find it first. Finding a hobby isn't a hard thing; just look around you, try out things you've never done before and determine which of them interest you the most. Then that is your hobby.

After finding your hobby, the next stage is to keep doing it repeatedly. Remember that your hobby may be anything, just ensure that it is something you love doing. Sing some music and see if you love to do that, then sing more than regular.

It even gets more interesting if you love reading. Take this time to read more self-love and self-development books to keep your confidence level high while keeping your mind off the heartbreak. You can also read some exciting novels from your favorite authors for one or two hours. Whichever way you decide to go, you should try a few titles: The Power of Positive Thinking by Dr. Norman Vincent Peale, Thrive by Arianna Huffington, I Am Malala by Malala Yousafzai.

"Hobbies can also increase your confidence level; by completing a particular task, you tend to feel in control; this may also decrease depression and makes you feel good. To achieve better results, try out things that make you feel good about yourself. Your hobbies do not

necessarily need to be reading or singing. Just something you love doing. How about learning a new language, traveling alone, trying out new recipes?"

• Improve your general outlook

There is a common habit among ladies going through heartbreak, and that is not looking good. Generally, when someone does not love you back, you tend to feel lost and start doubting yourself. You keep wondering if you do not look good enough for him. However, the answer is not within you, because you are a beautiful woman and you've got to appreciate yourself and look good every day.

"Just because someone does not love you does not mean you should give up on your look. Take time when dressing up, do not rush it. Looking good will give you the confidence you need to get through your day. Complement yourself and believe in your beautiful appearance."

Psychologically, women who dress well and look good exhibit a level of confidence similar to nothing. Knowing that you are looking pretty has a lot to do with how you feel about yourself the whole day. Hence, endeavor to dress well.

There is a widespread belief that changing your hairstyle means you are done with a toxic relationship or ready to move on. However, the inherent truth to that belief is that changing your hairstyle makes gives you an entirely new look that may be perfect for the moment. Go to the salon to make nice hair, wear some makeup after your skincare regimen and look super gorgeous for your outing or work.

It is even more important to improve your look if your crush attends the same school as yours or works in the same office. You do not want to see him looking happy for not being with you. Instead, make him regret choosing not to be with you. Start by looking good, and you start to feel good about yourself. Even at your lowest time, dress well, and when someone compliments you, suddenly you will realize that your self-esteem is at its peak again. This will reassure you of how amazing and positive you are.

• **Accept your negative emotions**

When you are hurting from heartbreak, you start to feel emotionally drained. It becomes tough to keep believing in the good things. Moment of self-doubt will begin to set in. I have learned that it is better to accept those feelings than prove yourself otherwise. This will help you contain your energy.

The first thing is to feel rejected. It is tough to deal with the fact that someone rejected you. You start asking if that means you are not beautiful enough or if it means you are not good enough. All of these feelings are wrong, but it may be hard to believe that they are wrong at the moment.

Instead of constantly asking questions, make peace with the fact that someone did reject you. If it hurts so bad, remember that you need to get better and become a better version of yourself.

Your negative thought and emotion should not end with you alone. It is natural to want to hate the person that breaks your heart. You will likely look for how to blame them, and you will find a reason to see them as bad people. If you feel this way, it is also acceptable. Try to reconcile with your feelings at this stage. Learn to accept whatever you feel. Even though anger is not good for you, controlling it may keep you bottled up for long.

Understand this feeling is not going to remain forever. Even if you find your fault, you will soon realize that it was not about you. This is just the moment you need to heal.

- **Meet new people**

Meeting new people has a way of making you happy. Naturally, new people come with new ideas. They tell you about the things you do not know about, and you get to them about your experience. Spending time with such a person may become regular, which can keep your mind off many things.

There are a lot of ways to meet new people. Going about your daily life is more than enough. Don't just go to the gym. Spend that with people there. Join a book club physically and online and volunteer for new organizations. You will meet a lot of new people doing this. You will find some more comfortable. Try being friends with them, exchange ideas, and before you know it, you are already done with your day.

Do not underestimate the impact a new person can have on your life. More time, we find out that we open up more to a stranger than an old friend. Talk to them about new things, about feelings and learn more about them too.

• Change your common routine schedules

Believe me, it takes more than what you see in movies to move on. It is not going to be a happy ending always, and you may not be moving straight into a better relationship, but it is an experience we all can't escape. Sometimes, you find out it is worth letting go than trying too hard.

Getting over someone takes more than those adage sayings and motivational speeches, or do you get better after hearing this? "Love is giving, not necessarily getting something back." Though healing from heartbreak is not the same for everyone, quitting what makes you closer to him is a universal rule.

Moving from one relationship to another doesn't mean that you are doing anything wrong; it is just the natural thing that happens till we finally meet the right person. Then, when the right guy comes along, you will realize it is worth the entire wait.

Nobody knows how you specifically feel; sometimes, you fall too hard than others, and sometimes it is just a fling. However, developing the will and the strength to move on is one of the ways to contain your feelings and live a better life.

If you are interested in moving from unrequited love and heartbreak, going back to your repeated daily activities may not be the best thing to do. I do not mean eating breakfast and packing lunch, and I also do not mean any of the steps already discussed in this book. I meant those things you do regularly to get closer to him and the things you do every day to make it work. You need to drop them.

- **Go on vacation/ appreciate nature for what it is (spend your weekend at the beach on vacation to somewhere lovely.)**

Immediately after your breakup, it is normal to want to grieve, and it is normal to spend some time alone fathoming your thoughts, feelings, and looking for a way to move on. But moving on is not a simple or ordinary thing. The pain we experience during heartbreak is found in a phrase in the medical field, and it is referred to as 'Broken Heart Syndrome.' It represents the heart aching, angry and sad feeling that comes along when we leave a relationship or set to move on from unrequited love.

Taking time to grieve should come with the desire to heal. However, healing won't come on your bed, nor will you find it on the couch; you've got to go out there and see things differently. Experience life and enjoy it to the fullest.

I was once terribly heartbroken. It did feel like nothing was going to heal me. Everything seemed off. Even though I decided to move one, I didn't achieve much by merely making that decision. I never realized it wouldn't come ordinarily because of my intention. The heart does not listen to what I have to say nor pity the pain I was going through. It kept hurting me bad. I couldn't give in, I was only 19 years, and I have a whole life before me. I couldn't afford to lose myself or stop believing in my ability. I had it rough then but had to get ready for college and get my life back on track. Everyone pitied me, I will read halfway and sleep halfway, but it doesn't seem to be enough help. I can still imagine how bad my stomach hurt like I was kicked in the gut. I lived this bad for a month. My mom couldn't bear to watch me waste away. Regularly she would check up on me and prepare breakfast, which didn't do much as well. One day she suggested that I take a trip on my own. That came unnecessary, and I didn't see why I should carry my sad life to meet new people or see something good. I didn't see how seeing the river flowing or admiring some artifacts would help me heal, but I want to get away from my life. So, I agreed to take a trip.

I left home after a week of getting myself ready, took the train, and I was already in Hawaii. The air feels different, and the atmosphere did a lot of good on the very first day. Interestingly it was my first time in Hawaii, and I already loved it.

I gave myself to the moment, and suddenly I could live as if nothing is bothering me before. I met different first-timers like me, and it was all fun spending time with them. What baffles me is how fast this was helping me, how easily I was smiling, and how much my stomach was free again. I feel differently alive.

That is the positive energy I needed; I want to spend more days. I want to live on the beach and keep experience this tropical environment. While I couldn't do it, I realized how much living a happy life is, how important it is to let go of my pain and live in the moment. I found happiness again, and back in Washington, I really couldn't appreciate that enough.

Travelling is probably the quickest and the easiest way to rise above all sorrow and smile easily. Touring different places makes the world looks entirely different to you, and sooner enough, you realize nothing is worth giving up for. You will want to live to see more of that. Appreciating nature will wake an awesome personality in your; it will give you the strength to smile effortlessly and slowly, the rivers will wash away your pain.

You need to understand that the end of a relationship is not a failure, no matter what your role is in the relationship. Use the period to grow your strength and self-belief. Take time out to know yourself better. Whether you are young or old, learn new things about yourself, teach yourself more, and create better standards. Even if you have anything to do with what happened, do not blame yourself, instead focus on improving yourself.

Naturally, you are angry about what happened, but this is not just anger; it is a time to heal and let out the emotions.

However, you need to control those anger and understand breaking up doesn't necessarily mean someone hates you; sometimes, it is what you need. If you initiate the breakup or decide to move on yourself, you may be angry at yourself. Do not hurt or hate yourself. Believe in your judgment; understand that no one knows you better than yourself. So, if it doesn't feel right, then it is not right.

Looking back on the things that cause you pain won't help you heal. Fantasying about how amazing your crush or ex-boyfriend is won't give you more joy; it will only make you want him more. So do away with the habit of remembering the past. This may not be immediate because we all have the habit of looking back on what we had and imagining what would have been. However, there are things you cannot control, and this may happen for the best.

It is ok to recall the memories but do not dwell in them. Bad memories may appear like it is helping you heal, but in the real sense, it will keep the creating the holes and hopes that makes you love the person more and want to get back together. It will make you want to check upon them. Either to know how good they are doing or how bad their lives have become after breaking up with you. However, no matter the result you find, it will draw you more closely to them. If he is doing fine in the relationship or after you express how you feel to him, you may even want to hurt him.

Constantly checking on your ex-boyfriend or your crush will drag the process of moving on down. If you check him up on social media, you need to quit doing that because it will keep bringing into the life he is living and what he is going through. In my experience, this never works out well. No matter what you see, the result will still hurt you.

If your boyfriend now has a new girlfriend, you will hate the girl, and it will hurt you because it means that he has moved on while you are still drooling over the relationship. Finding out that he is not living well won't do you any good either; you are either drawn to him or regretting making him go through that even though it is not your fault. For the moment, the best decision is to do away with whatever it is that is drawing you near to him.

• **Do Appreciate the Good Memories**

Sometimes what happened is not a lack of love but the inability to withstand all trials. It is the inability of one or both parties to keep trying, or the love is not worth fighting for. This does not mean you had it all painful. Your crush may be your friend, and it may even be that he is someone with a good personality. That he does not accept your feeling may not mean that he hates you or that he is a very bad person. Sometimes, the situation is not right.

However, when you look back on things, you may realize how amazing he is and how having him around makes a lot of sense. Do not be tempted to get back together or keep trying, but you can keep the good memories with you. Though this may be comforting, it may also make you feel empty, and you may start wanting him again. This is where you need to remember what happened. You need to understand that if two people couldn't make it work the first time, it is because there is a reason, and time isn't going to change that. Appreciate the good memories and learn to move on from them.

Fourth Week: Back with your emotion? Combine the steps below with the previous one in the earlier steps

STAGE 6

View the bigger picture

"

Try to look at the matter from the perspective of
another individual. The larger a picture you view
depends on the more perspectives you encounter.
Consider how his rejection may affect you later, next
week, next year, etc. Is his absence going to influence
anything in a year now? Broaden your vision of the
issue by examining from various points of view and
thinking about whether and how much more not
having him will continue to influence (and impact) you
down the line.

A guy who rejected you outrightly may never share your
dream of an ideal relationship, and he may never
comprehend your long-term vision and goals in a
relationship. Not letting the past affect you will be of great
help, obscure your view of the bigger picture; no matter how
dirty, how bad, how disappointing it has been, the future
holds better prospects. Focus on this bigger picture of the
new future.

Take the lesson and close the book; accept this as the end of
a chapter. You can't go back and write it back, but the future

is in your grip. This does not mean the end of your world or the end of your life. It means you continue on your trip. It would help if you permitted the bigger picture in your inner mind, and this gives a necessary chance for time to perfect the healing process.

Charles Dicken once said, "Reflect upon your present blessings, of which every man has plenty; not on your past misfortunes, of which all men have some."

Enjoy the beauty around you and appreciate what you have. This is how to view the bigger picture of life. You won't let unpleasant memories of his rejection hinder a good and insightful view of your existence. They will instead educate you to perceive the shades of life clearly. In essence, understanding the broad picture requires retroactive thinking about our response's short-term and long-term effects during critical periods such as this. So, it works: If for instance, the guy sent you his response through an email, move away before you reply. If a family member or a friend does something annoying, take a moment before you react.

• Count the possible downside (Time to see things you do not like about him)

Many people struggle to tap into optimism, and accept impossibility to wind a silver lining during periods of crisis. It is more like attempting to seek the good side of a bad coin instead of seeing it as the end of the World. Loving someone who does not love you will certainly assist you in realizing what your priorities should be. You will never invest so much effort into someone that is not worth it, and it will make you understand that it's always important to love yourself rather than anybody else. No matter how much you've fantasied about him, no matter how great he appears, you must bear in mind that nobody is perfect, and they aren't exempted. Every man has his downside, he could have appeared to be the best man you ever met, or you might think you'll never meet a person as funny, as understanding, mature or fun to be with as them.

The fact is that no man has it all. It is impossible to find a faultless person; in the heat of passion, you might have overlooked or underestimated some factors that reveal his dark or bad side. This is the reason behind the old sayings "love is blind." It would help if you also remembered that men could be deceptive and subtle too; in fact, he could have purposely hidden some facts from you. For example, his decision to stop dating you was not reached in a rush; he has cooked, contemplated, and meditated on it before arriving at his conclusion. He had probably kept so many facts from you immediately he made the decision not to date you. You need to emerge beyond the cloud of emotions and be logical for a while. Is he your boss? You can't mix business with emotion, and it affects workplace productivity. Consider the irreconcilable differences you felt you could cope with, its chance to break loose for a better person.

"We always have this mental image of your dream man, so here this is the time to check the

list and see how woefully he failed. Fathom if he fit in 100%, which is impossible."

Concentrate on his shortcomings rather than the happy times you shared. You may have thought that you shared laughter as well as fun with him; instead, remember the horrible times. Remember when he was rude to you, or probably made you cry, or how selfish he was generally. Think about how you don't like this individual. List their bad features and how they're not suited for you. The first thing on the list? Your emotional desires are not reciprocated. Both people must have invested in a working for the relationship. You deserve a person who truly wants to be around you, not somebody who does not want to be with you. Put anything on the list that you can remember, since it's only for you to get better.

Remembering the fault of someone you love can be hard at first; you have this picture-perfect image in your head. Hence, looking for his bad habit could be more challenging, depending on how much you know him. Perhaps he is somebody from a distance you have admired at work, or perhaps he is an old acquaintance that you have formed sentiments over the years. In any case, it might be beneficial for you in your quest to overcome this suffering to make a list of your desirable traits that this individual does not have. It not only helps you to humanize this individual, but it can also help you evaluate the characteristics you may wish to avoid in future partners rather than the romanticized picture you have in your brain. Our view is distorted by love, so it is really possible that you can perceive just the positive aspects of the person you like. Try seeing and recognizing his defects to remind yourself that he is not flawless. You can quit being obsessed by doing that. Say aloud some of the faults that you noticed. It might sound, "The way he calls back is awful. Moreover, I'm angry because his clothing never matches." Avoid placing him on a high pedestal since this may lead to long-term obsession.

Just write it down! Write it down! Studies indicate that understanding the worse traits of someone might help you overcome rejection more quickly. Convince yourself why such a relationship is wrong. The individual in issue may honestly be a nice guy, but it doesn't imply that you both are compatible. Persuade yourself of the error that would characterize such a partnership. Identify why the connection is probably going to end in a breakup. Incompatible objectives or beliefs are frequently an appropriate starting point. This may be very useful, especially if you both are close friends, and after a relationship breakdown, you may put an end to your friendship with the other person. Making you lose on both ends.

- **Realize that you are better off (Focusing on your self-worth and how beautiful you are)**

You need to realize your self-worth, focus on yourself and beauty. Not all men admire beauty because it takes one to know one. The reason why he rejected your proposal in the first place could have been that he realize how sophisticated you are. The truth is that people don't always reject your love base on negative reasons; for instance, you could have some values he doesn't share, like honesty and integrity, and a liar will always be scared of walking with the truth. He could be scared of you finding out his weaknesses, which is even a red flag. True love doesn't hide weaknesses, and true love involves the ability to accommodate each other's weaknesses. Only a cunning partner will try to hide away his weaknesses, and believe me, dating such a person can be toxic.

"If he cannot appreciate who you are, and this should push you to appreciate yourself. If he feels inferior, it is not your fault. You do want a partner that suffers inferiority complex. You need a man that is bold and competent, not a fidgety partner who gets scared of your values, and you need a man who would be supportive of your values and bring out the best in you."

- **Avoid blame game**

It is very natural in humans to place blame. When you don't get what you want in life, you get the natural impulse to place the fault in something or someone. Nobody loves to blame, yet at times, you find yourself blaming yourself. Resist the urge to blame either him or yourself if, in this case, it just couldn't work out. It is far better this way than getting trapped with an abusive or toxic guy. Tackle it head-on by not playing the blame game.

"Blame has a way of getting you trapped in permanent pain, and it makes you obscure to the reality on the

ground. You start seeing faults where there was none, and it takes no time for regret to set it; you start regretting the unknown. What if you had taken things slowly? What if you didn't communicate your feelings to them? A myriad of what-ifs starts to haunt your thoughts."

In no time, this will affect your overall health. Also, by criticizing the decisions, misjudgment will set in. You might reach a stage where you even start condemning the guys' sincerity. Remember that you're meant to appreciate the fact that he came out plain about your incompatibility. He could have decided to use and dump you, but instead, he was sincere with you. Therefore, placing blames will not make you see the positive side to all these.

Instead of placing blames try positive confessions. The more positive you sound, the more impotent you render the tendency to blame. Life is never a bed of roses, and life is full of ups and downs. You may speak out loud to yourself, and you need to convince your mind to accept it as part of the regular hazards of life. Don't ever believe it was something you're meant to do or that it was your irresponsibility that caused what happened.

If you love someone, you never have a 100% chance they will love you back. Sometimes you have to trust your feelings and realize you might have been wrong about things, and it's all right. Nobody is above mistakes, and you don't crucify yourself when this happen because they are bound to happen. I promise there's also a lot of mistakes in him if he's a human being. Think about it, if you have to think at all about it. Avoid thinking in rose-colored glasses. Look back objectively and see all the reasons and how this would not work; there have to be some because he'll be with you if he were the right person for you!

- **Recognize where you may have got it wrong**

It is crucial to separate blaming yourself from recognizing what could be wrong. Understanding the difference between the two will make you a better person without hurting your self-esteem.

You have no reason to blame yourself for loving someone who isn't reciprocating. However, knowing why you are not suitable for him or why he is not right for you will help you settle the score and move on quickly. I remember dating a friend during my first year in college; we really ended up loving each other and what started as a mere friendship turns into something perfect. I had it all going well, and he is just an ideal person for me. However, I knew nothing about his genotype. I stumbled on his health report one day and realized we just couldn't be together – He is AS, and I am AS too. I kept it all up, and I didn't want to tell him about it. After weeks of thinking alone, I just couldn't get the thought of getting pregnant for him mistakenly. I mean, I understand I was probably young for unprotected sex, but I really do love him. I opened up and told him my genotype, and it gets all sad and heart-wrenching. No one knew the right words to say; we were both devastated. In the long run, we had to get logical about the situation. The heart loves, but the brain has gotten some work to do.

In your situation, it is not necessarily your genotype. It could be any other thing. Simple acts of incompatibility are enough to make you see the reason why the idea of being with the person is genuinely wrong. Taking time out to fathom the things that are not meant to be will help get things in better perspective and understand this is probably for the best.

Sometimes what is wrong does not need to be an act of incompatibility; it may even be essential traits that the other person does not like in you. Recognizing this without blaming yourself will help you become a better person.

Dating coach expert Myles Scott put it: "Small mistakes and bad habits can lead to fear, doubt, and trust issues." It could have been that you were not mindful of your reactions when you made mistakes, which might have created doubt of your love and commitment level to the guy.

Scott further noted that "Too many bad things can build up and cause uncertainty...." For example, one general mistake ladies tend to make is banking on the assumption that they know what a guy is thinking or how he feels. Therefore, they may take his friendly outlook as evidence of his love for them, whereas he may just take it to be a casual intimate friendship.

Even though mind-reading may appear innocent, it carries some pretty bad consequences.

Another thing that turns guys off is if you only vocalize your opinion and act as though their opinion doesn't matter. Jokes about a guy's past or appearance, especially things he can't change, could also be a factor. Your intention might have been good or just to appear funny, but if it fell on a subject in which he feels insecure, then it's instrumental enough to hurt his feelings. Also, if you spoke too much about your past, telling them how bad your ex-was or how good you were and how it was all the fault of your ex, even though you intend this will make them think positive of you, it will achieve the direct opposite. It will make you appear to him as someone who doesn't let go of the past or someone who would find it difficult to forgive him. Even if your comments about your ex were too optimistic, it might spook him into thinking he probably isn't as good as your ex and wouldn't be able to satisfy you like him; if you break up with him, then what's the point for them to stick around. No matter how pressed you felt like talking, he and your ex were two different people, and you shouldn't punish him with the sad long stories of your time with your ex.

Kelsey M. Latimer, Ph.D., CEDS-S, psychologist, and founder of Hello Goodlife, commented that "I think the biggest thing someone can do to impact their relationship negatively is to be open about their partner's business without knowing what their boundaries are around personal information.". This deals with personality differences, probably he is an introvert who loves to keep his private matters to himself and got scared that being all out might expose him to unwanted attention. It is good to study and mirror the core personality traits of people we love. No one would blame him for rejecting you based on the incompatibility of your personalities; in this wise, perhaps the story might have been different if you have exercised more diligence. What you should do now is accept your fault and not resort to blaming yourself; whatever it was you got wrong, it is too late to change it now.

- **Take this as inspiration rather than rejection**

As stated earlier, nobody has the right to reject you as a person. So, when your crush turns you down, what he did was merely rejecting your proposal. Probably for reasons best known to him or apparent to you also. This should not be a source of depression for you, but motivation. It should trigger you towards self-improvement. If you allow rejection to get to you, depression may set in, laying the groundwork for suicidal thoughts, and your health might deteriorate.

According to psychologists, you must permit the expression of your feelings, you could be sad, and you may appear bleak, but never become your feeling. Never allow this sadness to lay hostage to your life. Lessons learned should serve as a stepping stone in future interaction with guys.

The truth is that tough times never last, but tough people do; no bad time in life is infinite; just stay strong the time passes. Your friends and relatives already heard about this, and a lot of them are telling you it is going to be okay, but you doubt this deep inside you, you feel you might never get over this, but I can assure you that you will, but the great news is that you will emerge stronger and wiser, all the guy did was sharpen your brilliance and bravery. It's like a storm you've learned how to ride; a repeat of the storm cannot make you sink again. Getting rejected can be as painful as getting a punch to the throat, but when the pain is over, you become immune.

- **Don't hold other guys to his standard/ stay open to new possibilities**

Not all guys are the same, and you never may know the right one for you. Even though the last guy rejected your love proposal, it does not mean every other guy you meet will behave like him. If you decide to treat every other guy with suspicion and are not open-minded, you won't realize when the right one will finally pass by. The pain of the last rejection can make you rigid in your future encounter with another guys, but ultimately this is not needed. All you have to do is to make sure you utilize the lessons learned from the last encounter. If you live in the belief that you will always be rejected, you are setting yourself up for more rejections. Therefore, it is good to give other guys the benefit of the doubt, a chance to prove the fact that not all guys are made of similar stock.

It might also be that when you started meeting guys again, all they give you is mixed signals, and it seems they are playing with your head. The fact is that immediately you start to believe that all men are the same, you are also accepting it. Probably the guy who rejected you made a lot of promises to you, you must know that he could have innocently done that in the spirit of true friendship. You could be the one who gave his promises romantic form, as such, you shouldn't tag all guys as liars because of that.

All you have to do is try different guys. If all guys are bad, what of your friends who currently have excellent friendship with? You may blame the guys for anything that you want, however at the end of the day, you decide the sorts of guys you end up with. The adventure, not consistency, appeals to you. You find a normal healthy relationship boring. You want to be thrilled. This way, you may never find a guy who will devote themselves himself to you. Hence, you need to set your priority right.

You must know that there are men out there whom you are the perfect spec for, one who would feel amazing to have you and will be satisfied you're more than enough for them. Any guy who thinks you're not good enough is the one who can't hit your standard because only mean people think this way.

The bottom line is that not all guys are heartbreakers. The fact that the last guy broke your heart, or every guy has broken your heart so far by constant rejection, but that doesn't mean every guy will continue to disappoint you. You deserve to be happy, and sooner than expected, you will be out there again with someone who genuinely values you and want to spend quality time with you and maybe the rest of his life too. So do not stop believing that life has the best surprises for you.

• **Do not forget your daily exercise (5:30 pm – 7 pm)**

Exercise may be considered a treatment and is powerful. Yes, dragging yourself to the gym during this period might be irritating, but it's always worth it, and you will always be so happy after it. Working out and sweating create endorphins, which are hormones that make you feel good, relieve tension, and have many other advantages. You know how important exercise is to your happiness and wellness.

You need to go and work out. Exercise boosts your mood. It can also keep you busy so that you have no time to keep obsessing about a guy who might not even care how you feel. It is excellent to make a suitable schedule for your exercise. Exercise helps clear the mind from myriad thoughts, and you cannot afford to concentrate on anything else apart from breathing and moving while you are so focused on pushing your body. Take a run, swim, bike, or another exercise that may both enhance your intellect and de-junk.

• **Do not forget your book (one to two hours daily)**

An excellent book might be a source of tremendous consolation if you are going through a breakup. You can escape fixation, but not in an unconscious way. The insights assist you to progress in your healing process; while you are completely absorbed, there is no chance for painful thoughts to cloud your mind. You may feel less alone if you know that others have had similar situations and come out on the other side. You can also get validation and help in processing your feelings by reading a book or listening to a podcast on your unique loss.

I remember getting through tough times with some of the books below

Tiny beautiful thing by best-selling author Chery Strayed, where she stated: "You don't need those people. By stepping aside, they've done you a favor. Because what you've got left after the fools have departed are the old souls and the true hearts. Those are the uber-cool sparkle rocket mind blowers we're after. Those are the people worthy of your love." You can get a copy online or visit any bookshop near you. Another author I would recommend is Juliet Milagros Palante, and she is the discerning, brilliant voice that can appeal to you right after a breakup. One of her key points I love best is: "You're going to encounter individuals you love who continuously screw up with you. You're going to learn to weed the warriors from the assholes. You will know which group of people you want to keep away from because you do not have safe zones for your heart. You will learn to forgive human mistakes and to remove the unfit."

Another book I truly enjoy is **"The Curse of the Boyfriend Sweater," by Alana Okun** and my favorite line from it says: "Just as I did not know what it was to be loved, I did not know that the others might quit loving you. And he informed me that one night at his house, he was sorry, but he was willing to break up. I did not feel so much sorrow as a shock at that time - that wasn't the norm. He was meant to stay with my squad, to be my person, and not just decide to go without providing me an opportunity to do so one day. What should I do with this whole emotion, this whole time, this space in myself that I was going to put aside for him? How can I return to myself?"

The next is "All about love" by Bell Hook, where he famously said: "One of the finest guidelines to how to love oneself is to give oneself the love that you frequently dream of getting from people. There was a period when I had ludicrous experiences with my over 40 body when I perceived myself as too overweight. However, I imagined that I would discover a partner who gave me the gift of being loved. It's stupid; don't I dream of someone else providing me the reception and assertion I rejected. At this time, the motto "You could never love someone if you cannot love yourself" was meaningful. And I add, "Don't expect anybody else you don't offer yourself to accept the love."

You can also try reading this **"Dear future boyfriend" by Cristin O'kefeeAptowicz.** The lines that readily come to mind are: "I can't quite believe I used to want to Sappho, Jason, I used to desire you I used to want you, Anaïs Nin and Henry Miller to Pablo Neruda. I wanted to be for you. I used to desire O for you to blow for you so that even the sails of

.

Odysseus could not bear it. But self-imposed ignorance is never a turn-on."

I will forever recommend this beautiful book by **Nora Ephron's "Heartburn,"** and our notable phrase is: "Sometimes I think love fades, but hope comes out forever. Sometimes I think hope disappears, but love comes forever. Occasionally I think sex plus guilt is comparable to love, and sometimes I feel sex plus guilt is equivalent to excellent sex. Occasionally I think love is as natural as the tides, and sometimes I think love is an act of will. Sometimes I think some people's love is better; sometimes, I think everyone fakes it. Sometimes I think love is vital, and sometimes I think that love is just necessary, else you would spend your whole time searching."

How about **"Once Ghosted Twice Shy" by Allysa Cole:** "He believed Fab broke his connection like a smartphone under a vehicle tire, but all their data was stored someplace on a cloud drive, he looked to be happy to download and ready to begin where they left off."

Lastly, I recommend **"In the dream house" by Carmen Maria**. It's a heartbreaking read that will make anyone who has been in a similar circumstance feel violently familiar with it. My favorite line of this excellent book is "A memory to remember: since grief has disappeared, but it does not mean that it was not once awfully. It just implies that time and space, beings of immeasurable size and compassion, stand between you two and keep you safe as they once could not."

In summary, it is time to begin to see the flickers of light at the end of the tunnel, don't remain where this ugly life circumstance of rejection has placed you, view the bigger picture, see beyond the current happenings, look at the good, bad and ugly, calculate your odd at both polar sides, good and bad, exercise daily, and if there were any fault of yours, accept and decide not to repeat it, read books that can uplift your spirit and gradually emerge, making your pain a stepping stone to greatness.

STAGE 7

Overall development

- Personal development

Learning and working on personal development is an unending process. It helps reassign and correctly identify ourselves. Its influence on healing is the ability to make you a person and expose you to more things that make life a better place for you. Your personal development after heartbroken can correct your mistakes and make you a more mature person.

This step entails taking proactive steps and control over your life. Understand that setting goals comes first, and working on getting them follows. So, identifying the aspect of your life that needs your attention is an excellent way to start.

Relationship sometimes draws us away from ourselves. You may later realize you are spending your time getting it to work, making him like you more than taking time to develop yourself. This is a bad thing to do to yourself; however, you may get carried away that you do not even notice it. Now that you are off the relationship, you heal from personal development.

It is easy to work on your development by learning about new self-empowerment and self-improvement skills. You only need to find things that are not entirely boring to you. Improving your knowledge about your skill, your job, or your profession will make you feel a lot more successful. Learning is not going to be an overall exciting process, but finding what you love can get you better. For example, conducting scientific research, learning, and reading about the new disease may interest you a document, and you may get so consumed by it that you forget all your pain. However, this will be a hilarious and worthless adventure for someone who loves to learn about writing a book. I enjoy international law, and I spend more time learning about what is happening around me. I just got interested in learning the histories of different countries and their political ways of life. Through it, I was learning, and I was getting satisfaction.

What Is Self-Development?

Through personal development and self-development are often used interchangeably; self-development entails focusing more on yourself and learning to know and appreciate yourself. Spending to develop a way to enjoy yourself will make you see the reason you are not a problem but a blessing. This brings in positive energy, which helps you get back on your feet in the long run.

It entails developing every aspect of your life, learning to let things go. Understanding your ability and becoming the best person you can be at the moment. It will make you see clearly, improve your knowledge about your personalities and also allow you to eliminate those thoughts and traits dragging you down.

Your self-development should not be restricted to reading; overall general self-development makes us better people. Even if it is unrelated to your profession or job, it may be something that makes you more socially inclined or that builds your character.

The benefits of personal development are limitless. It will help you define your life better. Sometimes, when we are heartbroken, the best way to deal with is to make rearrangement. Changing some things about yourself gives the reassurance that you will do better. This is what you can gain from improving yourself. But setting your vision right, you will be able to identify why those moments you spent regretting a broken relationship can be used to do something for yourself.

Personal development will also help improve your skills. Development is growth, and spending more time doing something new, exploring new things, and exceeding your boundaries will make you outgrow your usual self and learn new things about yourself.

○ **Learn new skills**

The benefits of learning a new skill should not be underestimated, especially when you find it hard to heal. Learning something new will be a worthwhile distraction, and selecting a course or skill that takes much longer can be more beneficial if you find out that moving on is getting a little too rough for you.

However, the focus of learning new skills is not to keep you distracted, and no one knew you are heartbroken when setting the skills. You can get a lot more from new skills. One of the excellent benefits is setting the right mindset. When you start learning something, you naturally find interest in it; it becomes something you want to focus on, unknowingly, you will be giving your mind and mind something else to think about.

Furthermore, learning something new is an excellent way to refresh the mind and boost your mental ability. Though we sometimes think refreshing the brain means freeing it from all thought and action. Focusing on a new skill may be the best way to free your mind of all the trouble you are currently going through.

"From my experience, learning something new without any form of pressure made me free my mind and gain more knowledge. In the long run, you realize it is time to get out there and do better."

You can choose to learn skills that are not directly connected to your career or job. Online courses where you can learn at your pace and in the comfort of your room will contribute immensely to moving on and forgetting your pain. Learning good communication skills will be overall self-improvement.

You get to express yourself adequately in front of people, which will save you more than your job. Similarly, the interpersonal skill will build your ability to retain friendship, identify when you are wrong, and learn to apologize; you will appreciate this when you find yourself in another relationship.

Learning about problem-resolving skills can even get you out of heartbreak, and this will also be helpful in different ways in life. Leadership skills will build your confidence and let you understand how to deal with pain.

The more you learn, the more you realize how more you need to know. Once you start satisfying the curiosity for more knowledge, it exposes you to a world where you can appreciate yourself better.

○ **Read books on self-development**
Do not stop reading even when you are done with the first book. Feed your brain with positive affirmations and knowledge

Reading is a way to pass the time and gain knowledge immensely. You do not need to pick up a book that gets you bored or all serious. In the course of writing this book, I have recommended more books to keep you busy, motivate you, and keep you going. You will find solitude in them. You find a way to sleep, and you will be surprised by how much you know and how many new ideas you experience. This period will somewhat be a blessing after reading extensively on several things in life. However, do not get unnecessarily serious. If you want to enjoy reading, it needs to be more fun.

Another way to read is to go for positive affirmations. There are thousands of books on how to keep reminding yourself of how amazing and unique you are. This may sound a little weird initially, but I can help but feel like a blessing after telling myself repeatedly. I also learned not to let anyone tells me otherwise. Now that is the energy you need to scale through this moment. Remember that I am rooting for you.

○ **Join voluntary organizations (an organization supporting feminism can help you grow and see your self-worth. Join online if physical ones are not near you)**

Another way to spend your time doing something productive is by joining organizations around you. As you are going through the phase of heartbreak and moving on, remember meeting new people and trying something new matters. You can meet new people and experience a new environment is by volunteering for organizations. I will significantly recommend joining an organization that helps with self-empowerment, overall development, mentoring, and feminism in general.

As a woman, speaking to another person will open the door to new experiences. We all understand what it means to listen to someone's pain without judging them; you will find comfort in some people and get inspired by their ideas and advice.

A friend shared her break-up experience with me, and I was impressed by how well joining a feminist organization helps her heal. It was a week after her boyfriend broke up with her, and all she had done was listening to music and watching movies, but whenever she is watching movies, she ends up seeing something that reminds her of the guy, and it is like breaking up all over again. Bad mouthing him with some of our friends didn't help as well; she somehow thought he is entirely flawless.

Nothing seems to work because she was so in love with a guy who doesn't love her back. Apparently, she fell in love with him and hoped he would find out somehow and then start their romantic relationship. It does not always end up this way. After declaring her love for him, she realized her crush was much in love with her other part, and there was no place for her precious feeling.

After a while, she realizes that trying those simple things won't help her; she needs something tasking, inspiring and educational. So, she started following TedTalk on YouTube. In her words, "I didn't know about feminism; I've always supported women going places but no first-hand experience. After listening to some TedTalk, I realize I need to know more about this wave, and I feel more like I belong there than sitting on my couch."

She started joining different feminist groups online; two of the groups are the Global Right for Women and Feminist Majority Foundation and performed some volunteering tasks. She would listen to her role model two hours a day, and it was very inspiring. She learned a lot of new things. It took an extra week to ultimately get back on her feet, but my girl came out with a different vibe and positive energy, and I loved it.

Feminism will teach you more than enough, and it will encourage you to stand up and do it better. There is a world full of opportunities and great people before you, and the only thing stopping you from experiencing something good and new is that you have yet to get over your crush.

"Feminism will make you see what the girl power looks like. Listening to people and sharing experiences will drive away fear and self-doubt. Assembling your thought to do something better and become part of a greater cause will stir up self-confidence and the ability to do away with your pain. In the long run, you will be stronger for pain and learn to deal with it."

You will also learn a lot about forgiving. At the same time, you will know enough about what is worth your time and tears. Trust me, and you will meet beautiful people who make your dreams seem so accurate and close. You start to meet people who are ready to hear you out and give you the strength you need.

○ **Exercise (5:30 pm – 7 pm regularly during the weekday; 8 am – 9:30 am during the weekends)**

If you are finding it hard to keep to your daily exercise, this may affect the progress of getting over your ex or crush. Tested by many, daily exercise is a way to freeing the mind of all stressful thoughts and ushering in a new breath of view. This mental effect will help boost your mood and increase the chance of moving on.

Certain things may be preventing you from focusing on your exercise. For example, you may feel like it is not worth it or that if your crush doesn't love, no one can. This self-doubt can make you see daily exercise as a waste of your energy. However, it is not true. Instead of giving up on your exercise, focus on achieving one body goal. After determining which body goal you want, examples are improving body shapes, reducing the waistline, or reducing tummy fat. Once you pick a goal, now draw up a regular schedule for the next 1 week. Try out a 7-day fat-reducing exercise. You can even go on YouTube to access the video and keep following it for 7 days. Watch how amazing you turn out.

If you do find losing body facts necessary, how about trying out some yoga positions. Suppose you already started focusing on simple yoga as recommended in the earlier part of this book. In that case, it is possible that you are getting fascinated about the various and healthy yoga position that you want to try more of it. However, if you are no longer finding the push to keep focusing on your exercise, getting a unique and new position will help you do it. You can try Yoga Plank for seven days to strengthen the body. You will need to repeat do this till you finally get the position right, and this is enough to take a week or two.

○ **Challenge unhelpful thoughts**

Heartbreak is one of the worst experiences humans go through. It will affect you physically and even mentally. Sometimes you become so restless that you do not even know you are losing yourself. Your mind will be thinking a lot, and the chances of thinking about what you did wrong are very high. We are in love. We really didn't see the other person's fault. We keep on thinking it is possible we failed to make it work out.

You start to think it was all your fault and that you probably made a mistake. Understand that it is ok to examine the facts and get it straight. It is also ok to take some blame only when you are wrong. However, you should stop having negative thoughts about yourself. Though it may still be hard to move on, reading till this part should make you understand that you are not the problem. The fact that someone didn't see you the way you wanted doesn't have anything to do with you.

Thinking you are worthless or undeserving of genuine love is also unfair to yourself. You need to deal with moving on with your strength. By now, you must have found out a lot about yourself, learn about new ideas, and experience differently. It is time to do away with negativity and focus your energy on staying healthy and positive again.

True love will find you, and when the right person comes by, you will find your attractiveness, uniqueness, and power. Till then, you need to be your primary source of strength.

Do not let a heartbreak keep you from progressing in your career; you definitely should not lose your job for this. Stay awake in your mind knowing what is yours will never pass you by.

The process may be rough; it may be hard to start believing another person. But do not give up. Take all the time you need, but do not wallow too long, for you deserve peace and love too.

Another negative thought is thinking you will never fall in love again. You see those people with a happy relationship; they didn't get there once. They experienced heartbreak before meeting the right person too. One thing I know that is certain is "Failure as any aspect of life isn't the end of the road; there are better chances ahead." If you do not experience heartbreak, it may be hard to know or appreciate true love. So, thinking you will not fall in love again or give anyone the chance to love you is the most painful torment you can make your heart go through. The heart will heal, it will heal over and over again, and when it is the right time, it will be an entirely different world.

In essence, no matter how bad it hurts and how much you want to give up on yourself, refrain from thoughts that make you think this phase won't end because it will, and after dealing with it, you will come out a stronger person.

- ## **Mental development**

Mental development does mean you need to be strong every time. When you are heartbroken, acting like the pain is not getting you and that you do not care about someone not loving you back is not going to give you a positive result. If at all you are getting something from that, it will be a heart that keeps breaking and misdirected emotions, so quit the strong acts.

Mental development is the habit of conditioning your mindset. It is more about understanding that moving on is the best option and doing your best to get your mindset on it. Naturally, when we are suffering through heartbreak, all thought of self-doubt starts to creep in. We constantly begin to doubt our ability and intention to be better people. When someone finds us imperfect, we sometimes become delusional and think we can be perfect. After a heartbreak, it is possible to feel like you are not enough. However, these negative thoughts aren't true about who you are.

Setting your mind right and developing your mindset is the best way to free yourself of unnecessary guilt and doubt. You may find it to see that you are wrong. Your ex might have manipulated you to see things the wrong way and made you believe you are the cause of the problem. However, learning to know that it is not your fault will take you a long way in the healing process. By identifying that what cannot be helped is not worth your time, you will feel healing from within.

By thinking about how to appreciate the merit of a healthy relationship, you will realize that spending time wallowing in pain is not what you want to do.

• **Physical development**

Physical development is everything and more. It is how you deal with your pain physically and how well you are able to contain your emotion, so you do not draw a pity party. Though it is better to have a friend over during a heartbreak, you do not want someone remembering what happens only when you are trying to move. Funny enough, when next you see those friends coming over to your place, you naturally move back to how well they were there for you when you were heartbroken, and then you remember who and what broke your heart. It is like repeating a cycle, but now is the time to move on.

Learning to deal with your pain can be painful in itself, and often we need those people around to get distracted and share ideas. However, the decision to move on needs you to be alone sometimes. It requires you to be strong for yourself and understand that your pain isn't going to stop you from living a better life.

Physical development prevents you from hurting people around you. When you are angry, you tend to attack everyone. Even the slightest thing makes you annoyed, and before you know it, you are already fighting with everyone, keeping grudges, and hating people around. It is very easy to transfer our anger when we are heartbroken because we need someone to blame. So, it is your friend's fault for not picking your calls; she had no reason to ignore your calls. It is more like the world is crumbling, and no one is saving you from it. However, this will only increase your anger and keep giving you a lot to heal from. It won't help you as you expect. It is no one's fault, and you have to start believing that.

So even if it feels like no one understands how bad it hurts, you do not need to say harsh words or mistreat anyone. Learn also to apologize if you've done this before. This will help you make peace, and in no time, you will find healing.

STAGE 8

Moving on: understanding the stages of grief

"

When you are heartbroken, it is ok to grieve. It is a natural response to unpalatable situations. Even if you do not know it, the sadness and pain you are experiencing after rejection are usually referred to as grief. The way people grief differs from one person to another. In reality, there is no hard and die rule to this, and it doesn't follow any specific or linear order. While grieving, you may lose your temper; you may cry; you may become angry; you may withdraw, feel empty. Know that what you are feeling right now is normal. It is essential to give yourself the chance to grieve, do not bottle up your emotions. Though people grief differently, there are some common symptoms in the stages of grief.

Grieving when you feel rejected is normal and natural; you may go through either all or some of the following stages as developed by A Swiss psychiatrist, Kübler-Ross; understanding these stages is critical to helping you through rejection and heartbreak easier. The stages are:

123

a. **Denial**

Denial is the stage that might help you get through the loss at the beginning. Having to deal with the caprices of life is more than enough. Hence, accepting rejection may become too overwhelming that you naturally want to deny it. You just won't want to accept the fact that he rejected your love. At this moment, it's normal to question how life will continue without him. You start to imagine what you both had or what you would have if your confession were accepted. This will block you from the truth.

For most people, it is hard to believe that, especially if the guy in question is your boyfriend and not a crush. You find it hard that someone you love so much is no longer feeling the same thing. Even if this had been an unrequited love, you want to tell yourself that it is ok as far as he gives you the chance to love him. The only persuasion you will get at this point is telling yourself that this is not possible.

You may think he is merely pranking you or probably testing your reaction—he must be joking or simply teasing you— it's just his funny self at play again. If you are told by a third party or receive it through email or text, you would believe it was probably meant for someone else. You do not live in "actual truth" at the denial stage but rather live in a "preferable" world, and you continue to hold on to your interest in him earnestly.

Though this may not seem like it, denial plays a significant role in helping you deal with heartbreak. The fact you didn't believe it will serve as a bit of consolation to keep moving. This is what you need to stand up again.

Denial helps to tackle your sorrow sensations. You refuse to accept, and this stands as immunity against its full impact on you at once, rather than becoming fully overcome with sadness. Think of it as "Hey; there is only so much I can handle immediately" as the response of the natural protection system of your body. As soon as the denial and shock pass, the process of healing commences. The truth is denial will help you deal with things, but it will not heal you entirely. At some points, you will need to deal with the truth and suppressed the lie within you.

b.   **Anger:**

As soon as you begin to live again in "actual" reality and not in "preferable" reality, rage might start to come. It's a usual stage for 'why me?' And "life is unfair to me!" You may want to blame people for your sadness and focus your anger on friends and relatives. You begin to find it hard to understand how such a thing may happen to you seems to you. Naturally, I believe this rage is a vital stage of grief.

"Though containing your emotions is good, at this stage, I encourage you to get angry as much as you want. It is necessary to experience the rage. Though it may seem like you've been in a continuous loop of rage, it will disappear -

but the faster you feel the anger, the faster it dissipates, and the faster you will recover."

Your sentiments of wrath - it's a normal response – and maybe a needed one, but not healthy. We usually have to manage our rage towards circumstances and people in everyday life. You may feel disconnected when you are in the grieving stage. All of a sudden, you find it hard to see your basis. Your life has crumbled, and nothing else to hang on to. Think of wrath as a binding force to reality. During this period, you may feel forsaken or neglected.

The benefit of feeling alone is that it may get you back on your feet again. You realize there is nobody, and you've got to take responsibility for yourself. Taking care of yourself; living an independent life becomes something you want to do.

This directing of rage, when channeled towards something or someone, might link you back to normal and connect you again to others. It is a natural "thing." It is something. It's a natural stage in healing, something to grab on to.

c.   **Bargaining:**

This will naturally follow the grieving stage. As you try to live like no one else has your back, you start to wonder if it is all worth it. You begin to consider trying for your love. It's more like his passion blinds you. The truth is you have nothing to be ashamed of, you are a great person capable of great love, and no one can be better than you. So, if you think you need healing in the first place, then this is the right feeling.

This stage is somewhat a negotiation stage. You were blinded faith or false hope; hence you start making all sorts of promises to him. You might erroneously assume through this; he will come back and continue or start a life with you again.

You are so anxious to return your lives to the way they were before the sorrow. Sometimes you are prepared to undertake a significant adjustment of life to please him. I was once ready to disable anything and everything to stay with my Ex.

If the fact that he is not responding to your promise and negotiation makes you feel guilt, it is okay. Though it is hard to see yourself at this stage, I will like you to understand that you did nothing wrong. However, I know the thought kept creeping in, and all you want to do is get a little consolation from taking responsibility for his lack of love.

You start to remember how many times you made him angry. Then you start finding your faults amid everything. Sometimes you blame yourself for not expressing your love sooner.

d.   Depression

Depression is a kind of grief that is generally recognized. Indeed, most people instantly link depression with sorrow because it is a "present" feeling. This depicts the emptiness we feel naturally when a loved one left. It is like living the reality we do not want. You might step back out of life, feel miserable, live in a fog at this time, and just want to sleep it off. The world may feel too daunting to face you. You would rather not be with others. You would not want to converse and have a sense of despair. You may even have suicidal thoughts — wondering, "so what is the point?"

e.   Acceptance

It's not that "it's all right he rejected me," but I'll be alright." Your emotions may start to stabilize at this time. You get back on the ground. The fact that the "new" reality is he'll never come back to love you – or that he might never have a rethink– is all right. It's not a good thing, but you can live with it. Indeed, this is a moment of change and re-examination. Crying, headache, sleeplessness, questioning the purpose of life, questioning your spiritual beliefs (e.g., your faith in God), feelings of detachment, isolation from friends and family, abnormal behavior, worry, anxiety, frustration, guilt, fatigue, anger, loss of appetite, and aches.

Medication, treatment and therapy are the most frequent ways to deal with grief. Your doctor may first prescribe medicine to help you work more fully. These might include prescriptions for sedatives, antidepressants, or anxiety to help you get through the day.

In my experience, support from your friends and relatives is the best treatment for grief. Rely on them, let them comfort, and give you words of encouragement. This is a valuable remedy when your situation creates problems in your daily life. In other words, you have difficulties working, and you need some help to get on track again. This is not to "heal" you of your loss but to assist you in coping effectively.

• Let out your grief/ write out a timeline of events / don't bottle up your pain

Journal therapy is the practice of writing your thoughts and emotions for therapeutic reasons, often known as writing therapy or therapeutic journals. It is a kind of individual therapy that lets you recognize your emotions, know their sources, and finally cope with them via frequent journaling. Try to put your thoughts and feelings on paper if you are not a natural sharer or are not prepared to speak. I believe it is useful when you write your thought down. Do not block how you feel; let your hand write as much as you like. This will help you put things in a good perspective.

In addition, keeping this record helps you observe how far you have progressed with your healing process.

Although journaling is beneficial, it is not a substitute but an addition to standard professional therapy. It's an occasion to gain a better understanding of yourself via writing. Reviewing your heartache can help you by separating yourself from the anguish you're feeling. It is a strong chance that can make you sense your own emotions and get them under control. In the story of your grief, you'll finally have a say. It will bring you out of negation. Bluntly approach your writing. Don't filter to look better, more intelligent, or stronger. Let everything out. Let it out. Be harsh if you want to be cruel, beg, sound weak, spill out whatever is inside you. If you have to use foul words, write them down as you feel it. Nobody's going to read it but you, so do not be scared of keeping it honest. Let the lines in your diary reflect your anger, denial, and anguish.

Write as if you are addressing the guy personally; it brings a lot of relief, believes me. Pain will come and pass in waves. You're going to feel good on certain days and may feel very bad on others.

Just write, don't force yourself to write only on your pleasant days. On the days you feel most terrible, try to write. This is how journaling can do the most for you. Letting loose of the thoughts caught up in your mind in times of distress is a great way to heal. Reading out your thoughts to yourself makes them appear natural; you can ultimately let them go if they're real. They will continue to annoy you for a more extended period if they linger in your brain. So, after penning your journal try to read it out loud to yourself.

- ## **Resist the temptation to turn to anger**

After rejection, it is common to feel upset. It is one of the main phases of grief. Hence it is often somewhat inevitable - regardless of form or magnitude. The anger generally starts as soon as the denial is released. You realize that it's over and that everything now feels genuine, and you can't do anything to alter it. Sometimes the anger masks the grief that eventually follows in an attempt to disguise it. It's your brain other times attempting to handle the circumstance. In any case, your health needs to cope with anger after a breakup! The issue is that anger is a kind of stress, while it is a helpful emotion in many respects. It can harm your adrenal and digestive system and create a weary you when you need to gather energy and focus on recovery.

You can control your anger by reminding yourself of the better prospects the future holds. The guy isn't the last guy on earth. Talk about your anger to friends and relatives and engage in activities that you love, try to vent your anger on something productive, play your favorite game at the most complex level, engage in something physical and yet productive, it has a way of gradually lifting you out of your angry state.

• Never turn to drugs or alcohol

Alcohol may impact your disposition; whether you're thrilled or depressed, alcohol can exaggerate your current mood. It is therefore not recommended to resort to alcohol intake after a guy rejects you. You need to be guarded and more aware of your emotions, and drinking alcohol may increase your chances of doing things you don't want to do, such as calling the person who rejected you, indulging in other drug-related behaviors, or getting involved in an unnecessary fight. If you don't take precautions, alcohol might aggravate your sadness and turn you into an addict. You might also develop an alcohol use problem, which raises your chances of abusing other substances. In the long run, you may end up doing more harm to your mental and emotional health than good. You should also consider the long-term health consequences of alcohol use on your kidneys and other essential organs. When the need to drink arises, you can satisfy it with wines and other non-alcoholic beverages.

You need to know that alcohol merely provides temporary comfort, and all your pains return when you become sober. Avoiding alcohol while managing emotional distress caused by heartbreak may feel stressful on its own; this added stress can increase your prompt to drink. This is normal, and exercising some self-care practices can help you manage this distress.

You can achieve this by giving priority to wellness. Feeling physically strong can equip you to confront the urge to drink. For instance, when you stop taking alcohol, you notice that you gain more physical strength. This strength has a way of inspiring you to keep up fit to withstand the pain you are going through.

If you are already sticking to no alcohol during your heartbreak, celebrate the progress. You can talk about it to friends; they will also encourage you, and the fear of them catching you drinking what you told them you're overcoming might be an added advantage.

You should also ensure that you stay hydrated, drink enough water. This is because if your body feels thirsty, it increases the likelihood of resorting to chilled alcoholic drinks, so as the general saying goes, prevention is better than cure. Kindly provide your body with adequate water.

It is also advised to add your progress on this to your journal and consult the journal regularly. Maybe you've gone 48 hours without alcohol, make a note of it and make sure it only gets better, motivate yourself with the accomplishments written in your journal.

The fact is no one loves an alcoholic; taking it will make your chances of meeting better people very slim. Constantly taking alcohol will not help you. It will only increase your depression and anxiety.

You should also make it clear to friends and relatives that drinking will never be permitted in your home and kindly turn down invitations to events where you're likely to be served alcohol, it is a gradual process, and with time, your heart will be completely healed.

• **Kill suicidal thoughts in the bud**

While it is natural to have some negative thoughts during such a difficult time, suicidal thoughts after a breakup should be avoided at all costs. You need to understand that time heals all wounds, and you will ultimately move on. If you don't kill suicidal thoughts immediately, it becomes more challenging to overcome them.

Rejection or breakup results in a higher level of stress, affecting our mental health and impair our ability to think correctly. In this situation, it is possible that you start to doubt the reason for your existence and wonder why living matters. It is understandable.

Remember that problems are for a moment while suicide is permanent, the damage is irreparable, suicide is a crime against yourself, against your maker.

Killing yourself or the thought of it is a lack of belief in your ability to do better and a valid statement that you do not love yourself. Ironically, you are not capable of loving people if you do not love yourself. This is not true because you are capable of amazing love, and the fact that you are heartbroken right now is a testimony of the great love and kindness existing within you.

So rather than loving someone, now is the time to think about self-love. Look in the mirror and see how wonderful and unique you are. No one, I mean no one looks exactly like. Do not deprive yourself and your loved ones of the chance of seeing you more often. Think of any reason to keep going. Even when you are tired, the slightest smile from your parents, friends, and siblings may be worth holding on to. So, remember the happy moments and believe that the slightest things count.

How about thinking of what life has in store for you. No matter your age or what you are going through right now, there are better days ahead, and believe me, this is not fluff. We all had terrible days; days we think the world is just designed against us. Days will start to doubt our ability to make it work again, and days will start to believe happiness and love are long gone. However, life surprises us with something bigger, telling us that we are part of a unique design. In our one little and seemingly unrecognizable way, we are making it work and pushing a greater cause forward. So, you cannot quit.

If the thoughts are constantly coming to your heart, make sure you destroy every dangerous material you might have access to, if you have some chemical at home, without second-guessing, throw it right away to somewhere you can never reach for it again, if you think too many dangerous materials surround you, leave your home immediately, go to a friend for some surprise visit, make sure you share with them what made you visit, I am very sure they will help.

Take note also if you are under any medication, certain drugs can increase the risk of suicide; visit your doctor and explain how you've been feeling. Never under any circumstance, keep this to yourself.

Always remember that the sadness you currently experience is nothing compared with what your loved ones will feel if you go ahead to commit suicide; if you think there's nobody that really cares, try your neighbor, or try contacting any emergency service with your phone. If you suddenly feel you can't bear the pain anymore, seek expert help.

Suicide often hides behind such feelings of hopelessness and distraught, but remember that beneath the black clouds is the bright sun. All it takes is time, and brightness will emerge.

- **Use music as a tool of mental relief/ choose songs with uplifting content**

After your heartbreak, are you still feeling the sensation of a massive hole residing in the bottom of your heart, with no prospect of healing? If yes, try listening to music

Music can be used as therapy during this period, and it is effective in decreasing pain, anxiety, and tension. In addition, science has proven that music can help heal a broken heart. There is a sense that you will never be able to recover from this sorrow, but science teaches us that there is a way out and that slowly with every chord played and every harmony that resonates, the shards of one's heart will begin to heal.

Grasping how music has such an impact on your emotions means you can use it for getting over an ex. Sadness induced by music has a function in well-being by giving comfort and moderating unpleasant emotions and feelings. So rather than thinking, 'I can't believe I was deceived that way,' music might make you realize better positivity about your future ambitions as well as other people who love you.

"While living through this rough patch, listening to your favorite artist songs and understanding how every word resonates with you makes you feel like you're not alone in your situation. Indeed, music is a tremendously efficient

method to feel connected with others and thereby overcome loneliness. The different musical components of rhythm, melody, harmony, and pace create a mental and affective reaction that includes the affective component of pain that helps to improve mood and healing."

Because a breakup is a loss, it elicits all of the emotions associated with loss: bewilderment, denial, yearning, rage, melancholy, and hopelessness. Heartbreak may intensify our needs for consolation, friendship, and empathy in the midst of all this upheaval music is indispensable.

The words of a great breakup song might help you convey emotions and feelings that are otherwise difficult to explain. You might not even realize how you feel until you hear it wonderfully expressed in a song. Hearing, "How the fuck can you repair a broken heart?" at such a moment when it might be challenging to coordinate your ideas, much less even convey them to others, can instantly offer your insight about the agony you've been suffering with: it's a shattered heart! A song's lyrics may bring untold and unknown ideas to light, bringing you nearer to knowing what is happening deep down. If you're just a listener, you may not understand the depth of the music and intensity, which could help take your mind off the current state. If you're a singer and listener, this is the next level of involvement wherein you'll understand not only the depth of music but also feel an inner connection to the message; the more you involve yourself with music, the more you'll get your mind off the breakup.

If you're a music-maker or play any instrument, this is the ultimate level of getting yourself involved with music that you forget about your pain. This is because song-making takes so much of your time and attention that you will not feel alone anymore. And that's the best part because you shouldn't be alone at this sad moment.

- ## You may consider adopting a pet

The confusion and loneliness that follows a guy rejecting you can make you suffer from depression, weight gain or loss, and solitude from relatives and friends. Fortunately, our animal pals may be the most devoted companions. Depression has a physical impact on health, but spending meaningful time with your animal buddy can reverse these effects. Cortisol, a stress hormone, decreases in your body. Interacting with animals also increases serotonin levels. Such chemical processes assist in alleviating mental discomfort right away. Any therapist will tell you that exercise may help you feel better. While I do not dispute that and even recommend it, I know that a dog or cat may yank you out of bed and make you face the day. Even rising to feed your cat may provide you with enough energy to shower, dress, and do some errands. Dogs and cats add structure to your day, which can boost your productivity significantly.

A pet will do you more good than you can imagine. For example, keeping your pet active by playing with a toy or taking a stroll helps boost serotonin and dopamine levels. These "feel-good chemicals" aid in healing a depressed heart and aid the treatment of severe mood disorders such as depression and bipolar disorder.

• Don't rush the process

Don't go into a healing relationship. I know you've heard that so many times, but I really want to tell you again. Though it is not a universal rule, not rushing into another relationship is meant to keep you safe and protect your heart. No one wants to imagine the idea of another heartbreak immediately after an earlier one. Take your time to heal.

I will like to remind you that you have the time to yourself. Maybe not eternally, but you do have the time and do not let anyone rush. If you meet someone new and he is ready for a relationship, make him understand where you are right now. All you need is the strength to heal, and you should not find that in another guy.

The truth is you deserve someone worth the wait and can wait for you too. So, if you receive a proposal from someone you love, it is ok to take things slow. Something like being a mere friend will do you more good without setting your hope too high. Let him walk with you at your pace, do not rush it. No one is worth rushing and hurting for. I really do not want you to be back where it all started.

"Don't go into another relationship too fast and believing you're OK. It's the finest fast cure out there, but you never truly get over your ex in three days. In the long run, you haven't truly moved on from your past, and when

your next relationship breaks, you'll have two exes to contend with. You're simply putting off the inevitable agony.''

Understand that this is not to advocate pessimism; it is to ensure that you heal first before getting into another relationship. I have come to understand that it is possible to find the right person immediately after heartbreak. You don't control the timing. However, if you are in this situation, you really want to be careful.

I won't recommend keeping him waiting for too long. Getting your facts straight will do a lot of good here. Take time to understand how much he cares about you. Do not idolize him, and don't get ahead of yourself. Kill the loving thought to see clearly, and more than any other tips, follow your heart.

Your intuition will hardly lead you to the wrong place, so if your heart wants it, then you probably want it too. Allowing the heart to lead is one way to love and appreciate life. You see, this heart makes many good decisions even if it is not as bright as your brain. But in a matter of love, the brain will fail you. Do not get too logical; how about following your heart and believing the process.

• **Indulge yourself in good diets:**

I tell people food is life, but most of them do not really understand me until they start some high-class chef meals, and it is all yummy. Delicious food makes you happy, and that feeling is just irreplaceable. If you are thinking I'm just a foodie, how about trying out some lovely recipes. Barbecue is a good place to start. You can also indulge yourself in some mouthwatering steaks.

Heartbreak or rejection can also take its toll on your health. Going through heartbreak or refusal naturally increases the level of your stress. Without working or doing anything serious, anger, depression, and sadness affect our mental health and physical capacities rendering us severely drained and highly exhausted. Eating more healthy fruits and meals will be beneficial for boosting our strength and suppressing anger. Consider eating almonds as regular snacks. You can also substitute a bowl of ice cream for a nicely prepared smoothie using several fruits and nuts. Below are some of the foods to help with the healing process

a. Almonds

Almond supplies the body with a higher level of zinc, vitamin E, and vitamin Bs. This will help significantly in assisting your body in dealing with and adjust to stress and anxiety. Almond can increase caloric- intake, but a moderate portion will be just fine.

b. Yogurt

Yogurt is good for the body and the skin. Replacing excess ice cream with yogurt will do a lot of good without depriving you of the sweet taste you may want to keep. I recommend trying Greek yogurt. The active and live cultures present in Greek yogurt will help a lot with stress. It will also release Tommy's pain. Chilled yogurt will relieve your mind and rejuvenate the body, and you will feel terrific. Yogurt also contains probiotics and protein, which will help with the digestive system and promote overall health.

c. Whole-Grain Cereal

Change the breakfast from staying hungry and remembering memories to bulking your stomach with some healthy grains. Cereals are really high in carbohydrates which will supply your body with the strength you lost thinking and sobbing. Food high in carbs will enhance the brain to release serotonin (the feel-good chemical), and this will help boost your spirit for the day. Combine whole-grain cereal with low-fat milk in other to give yourself something healthy.

d. Healthy recipes

Learning and trying out new recipes can keep you busy during the weekend. Spend time surfing the net for recipes that keep you all good, boost your immunity, maintain body weight, and improve your health. Remember, you've been through a lot, so taking time out to spoil yourself a little won't hurt anyone.

Aside from the fact that good and healthy recipes will assist your overall body system, they will also keep your mind off things. Cooking demands your 100% concentration; you do not want to hurt your hand or pour the oil in the wrong pot. So, when you decide to cook, be ready for it. Spend few hours on those meals and have a plate of something delicious and healthy for yourself.

If you are not a huge fan of cooking, trying a new restaurant will give a similar result, and you just got to get out of your bed, and see the sun shines brightly again. Give yourself a little pampering, order something you've always want to taste. Remember to eat healthy.

• **Date and meet new people**

We've already examined the benefits of meeting someone new. How about you date someone now? Dating someone else helps you forget the old love. Without necessarily waking the old memories, a relationship will give the closeness, intimacy, and quality time-spending that you enjoy with your ex or anticipated with your crush. This has a way of dealing with your heartbreak like it never really existed. You become so happy that you will naturally forget the pain the previous guy caused you. However, finding the courage the love again can be more challenging than you imagined. It may become hard to trust someone again. I explained why you should never treat other guys with his standard because not all guys come to break your heart.

When you meet someone new, it is good to take it slowly. Take your time to know the guy better before trusting him completely. Do not give up your heart easily or freely to someone else, but don't let the old love obstruct the growth of a new one. You are capable of falling in love again.

• **See a professional if you're unable to recover**

If letting out your grief to friends or family does not help, reach out to a therapist. A therapy session for healing is not bad at all. The idea of telling someone you really do not know all the pain you are going through has a way of allowing you to free your mind. It is a no-judgment area. Knowing that no one is judging you will make you tell the story of how it was and show where it hurts.

Also, therapists have a unique way of listening and connecting to you more profound than any friend. From the first session, you will begin to understand yourself properly. After few answer and question sessions, you will learn to know where it all went wrong and what way is more suitable for your healing process.

Journaling will also help significantly in this regard. You may already write out all your pain but still find it hard to make peace with it. You can present this to your therapist to seek the best possible advice.

Interestingly, you do not need to go out for a therapy session. Though I recommend physical therapy as it may help you connect well to the person. Online therapy will do just fine. Find the time to check online to see if someone matches what you want.

Conclusion

The rejection or breakup isn't anyone's dream, but it happens for a reason. Though it is hard to see why your love life had to end or why your crush doesn't think it is a good idea to be with you, seeing the bigger picture and appreciating yourself for the capability to love is one way to heal probably.

Understand that your personality or who you are has nothing to do with the fact that someone cannot love you back. No one knows you more than yourself, so you've got to get the courage to appreciate your inner beauty as well as your strength. Admire the courage to go all out and tell him you love him and enjoy the gut it takes to reject your proposal. Life happens, and sometimes all we have remained is dealing with the broken pieces of reality. The earlier, the better; however, this is not a hard-and-die rule. No one has the right to tell you how to grieve or what to do. So, if it is taking you a little longer to heal, understand that you will get there, and some days, you feel like nothing happened.

Dealing with heartbreak and rejection differs from one person to another. For some of us, it is about watching some Hollywood movies, reading few books, and getting back on track, and for some, it is really a messy time, and being around people may even become a little annoying. The feeling of betrayal and rejection. Understanding someone you want badly didn't feel the same can be overwhelming, but we've all been there before, so I can tell you that you will be ok.

It is essential that before you set up for love, you build your self-esteem and self-confidence. Learn to understand those things that make you an incredible and unique person. See your own value. With this in place, you will be able to handle heartbreak boldly. It won't always end with smiles, but even a disappointment is sometimes a blessing in disguise. This time will pass, and when the time is right, you will whole and wonderful again.

Finally, if you enjoyed this book, please let me know your thoughts with a short review on Amazon. All that you need to do is to click the blue link next to the yellow stars that says "customer reviews." You'll then see a gray button that says "Write a customer review"—click that and you're good to go. It means a lot, thank you!

Eliza

www.ingramcontent.com/pod-product-compliance
Lightning Source LLC
Chambersburg PA
CBHW071004120626
46546CB00003B/928